The Everyday Chef

DESSERTS

Celebrity Press • Nashville, Tennessee

Text copyright © 1997 by Hambleton-Hill Publishing, Inc.
Some or all of the photographic images in this book were provided by
Digital Stock, Corporation 1-800-545-4514

All rights reserved. No part of this publication may be reproduced or transmitted
in any form or by any means, electronic or mechanical, including photocopy,
recording, or any information storage and retrieval system,
without permission in writing from the publisher.

Published by Celebrity Press
An imprint of Hambleton-Hill Publishing, Inc.
Nashville, Tennessee 37218

Printed and bound in the United States of America

ISBN 1-58029-017-5

10 9 8 7 6 5 4 3 2 1

The authors and publisher have made every effort in the preparation of this book to
ensure the accuracy of the information. However, the information in this book is
sold without warranty, either express or implied. Neither the authors nor
Hambleton-Hill Publishing, Inc. will be liable for any damages caused or
alleged to be caused directly, indirectly, incidentally, or consequentially
by the recipes or any other information in this book.

Graphic Design/Art Direction
John Laughlin

Contents

Cakes 5

Strawberries 15

Apples 19

Cobblers & Fruits 23

Pies 27

Cheesecakes & Tortes 37

Pastries 47

Ice Cream Creations 53

Cookies & Snack Cakes 57

Index 64

Conversion Table

Metric Conversions

1/8 teaspoon = .05 ml
1/4 teaspoon = 1 ml
1/2 teaspoon = 2 ml
1 teaspoon = 5 ml
1 tablespoon = 3 teaspoons = 15 ml
1/8 cup = 1 fluid ounce = 30 ml
1/4 cup = 2 fluid ounces = 60 ml
1/3 cup = 3 fluid ounces = 90 ml
1/2 cup = 4 fluid ounces = 120 ml
2/3 cup = 5 fluid ounces = 150 ml

3/4 cup = 6 fluid ounces = 180 ml
1 cup = 8 fluid ounces = 240 ml
2 cups = 1 pint = 480 ml
2 pints = 1 liter
1 quart = 1 liter
1/2 inch = 1.25 centimeters
1 inch = 2.5 centimeters
1 ounce = 30 grams
1 pound = 0.5 kilogram

Oven Temperatures

Fahrenheit	Celsius
250°F	120°C
275°F	140°C
300°F	150°C
325°F	160°C
350°F	180°C
375°F	190°C
400°F	200°C
425°F	220°C
450°F	230°C

Baking Dish Sizes

American	Metric
8-inch round baking dish	20-centimeter dish
9-inch round baking dish	23-centimeter dish
11 x 7 x 2-inch baking dish	28 x 18 x 4-centimeter dish
12 x 8 x 2-inch baking dish	30 x 19 x 5-centimeter dish
9 x 5 x 3-inch baking dish	23 x 13 x 6-centimeter dish
1 1/2-quart casserole	1.5-liter casserole
2-quart casserole	2-liter casserole

Cakes

Batter:
A thin mixture of flour and liquid that is combined with other ingredients to make foods such as cakes.

Beat:
To mix ingredients until smooth by using a quick stirring motion or an electric mixer.

Quick and Easy Chocolate Cake

1/2 c. self-rising flour
1/2 c. sugar
2 level tbsp. cocoa
pinch salt
1/4 c. butter, melted
1/2 c. milk
1 egg
1 tsp. vanilla extract

In a large mixing bowl, combine all ingredients in the order listed. Beat well for 2 minutes. Pour into a greased, 7-inch cake pan. Bake at 350°F for 35–40 minutes.

Chocolate Marshmallow Cake

1 1/2 c. flour
1 tbsp. cocoa
1 tsp. baking powder
1 tsp. baking soda
1/2 c. milk
1/4 lb. butter, softened
3/4 c. sugar
1 tbsp. golden syrup
1 egg, beaten
1/4 c. boiling water
marshmallow cream
1 container chocolate icing
chopped nuts (optional)

Preheat oven to 350°F. Grease 2 round cake pans. Sift together flour, cocoa, and baking powder; set aside. Dissolve baking soda in milk; set aside.

In a separate bowl, cream the butter and sugar. Add syrup and beaten egg; mixing well. Gradually add flour mixture alternating with milk mixture. Finally add the boiling water. Pour into prepared pans. Bake for 40 minutes, or until done.

When the cake is completely cool, place one layer on a serving platter and spread with marshmallow cream. Place the second layer on top. Ice with chocolate icing and sprinkle with chopped nuts.

Mississippi Mud Cake

1/2 c. butter, softened
1 c. sugar
3 large eggs
3/4 c. all-purpose flour
1/2 tsp. baking powder
dash salt
1/4 c. plus 2 tbsp. cocoa
1 tsp. vanilla extract
1 c. chopped pecans
10 oz. marshmallows
Chocolate Frosting (recipe follows)

Cream butter. Gradually add sugar, beating well. Add eggs, one at a time, beating well after each addition.

In a separate bowl, combine flour, baking powder, salt, and cocoa. Add the flour mixture to the butter mixture. Stir in vanilla extract and pecans. Spoon batter into a greased 13 x 9 x 2-inch glass baking dish. Bake at 325°F for 15–18 minutes, or until the top is barely soft to the touch.

Remove cake from oven and cover top with marshmallows. Return to the oven for 2 minutes, or until the marshmallows are soft. Spread marshmallows over cake and immediately cover with Chocolate Frosting. After frosting has hardened, cut cake into squares.

Chocolate Frosting:
1/4 c. butter, softened
1/4 c. plus 1 1/2 tbsp. cocoa
16 oz. confectioners' sugar, sifted
1/4 c. plus 3 tbsp. warm milk
1 tsp. vanilla extract

Cream the butter. Add cocoa, mixing well. Gradually beat in confectioners' sugar, adding warm milk as necessary, until frosting is of spreading consistency. Stir in vanilla extract. Spread immediately over warm marshmallows.

Peanut Butter and Chocolate Cake

2 c. flour
2 c. sugar
1/2 tsp. salt
1/2 c. butter or margarine
1 c. water
1/2 c. vegetable shortening
3 heaping tbsp. cocoa
2 eggs, beaten
1 tsp. baking soda
1/2 c. buttermilk
1 tsp. vanilla extract
2 tbsp. peanut butter
Icing (recipe follows)

Combine flour, sugar, and salt in a large mixing bowl; set aside.

Mix butter, water, shortening, and cocoa in a saucepan. Bring to a boil and pour over flour mixture, mixing well.

In a separate bowl, mix eggs, soda, buttermilk, and vanilla extract. Add to hot mixture; mixing well.

Pour batter into a greased and floured 9 x 13-inch pan. Bake at 350°F for 15–20 minutes. (Prepare icing while cake is baking).

Remove cake from oven, and, while it is still hot, spread a very thin layer of peanut butter over the top.

Immediately ice the cake.

Icing:
1/2 c. butter or margarine
3 heaping tbsp. cocoa
1 pkg. (16 oz.) confectioners' sugar
1 tsp. vanilla extract
1/2 c. chopped nuts (optional)
6 tbsp. milk

In a saucepan, melt the butter and cocoa, mixing well. Do not allow to boil. Remove from heat. Stir in confectioners' sugar, vanilla extract, and nuts. Add just enough milk to make the icing thin enough to spread. Mix well, and apply to cake while still hot.

German Chocolate Cake

4 oz. German sweet chocolate
1/2 c. boiling water
1 c. butter, softened
2 c. sugar
4 egg yolks
1 tsp. vanilla extract
2 1/2 c. flour
1 tsp. baking soda
1/2 tsp. salt
1 c. buttermilk
4 egg whites, stiffly beaten
Coconut Pecan Frosting (recipe follows)

Melt chocolate in boiling water.

Cream butter and sugar until light and fluffy. Add egg yolks, vanilla extract, and melted chocolate. Add dry ingredients alternately with buttermilk. Fold in egg whites.

Line three 9-inch baking pans with wax paper. Pour batter into pans, and bake at 350°F for 30–35 minutes. Allow cakes to cool, then remove from pans. Spread Coconut Pecan Frosting between layers and on top of cake, leaving sides unfrosted.

Coconut Pecan Frosting:
1 c. evaporated milk
1 c. sugar
3 egg yolks
1/2 c. butter
1 tsp. vanilla extract
1 1/3 c. flaked coconut
1 c. chopped pecans

In a saucepan, combine all ingredients except coconut and pecans. Cook over medium heat, stirring constantly, until mixture thickens, about 12 minutes. Remove from heat, and stir in coconut and pecans. Cool until spreadable.

Peanut Butter Spice Cake

1 tbsp. butter or margarine
1 c. creamy peanut butter
1 c. sugar
1 orange, grated peel only
3/4 c. orange juice, strained
2 1/4 c. plain flour
3 tsp. baking powder
1/2 tsp. baking soda
pinch salt
1/2 tsp. ground allspice
1/2 c. finely chopped walnuts
1/2 c. white raisins

Preheat oven to 350°F. Use 1 tablespoon butter to grease an 8-inch tube pan. Place pan in refrigerator until ready to use.

Combine peanut butter, sugar, and orange peel; beat for 10 minutes. Gradually beat in orange juice.

In a separate bowl, sift together flour, baking powder, soda, salt, and allspice. Fold into the peanut butter mixture. Stir in walnuts and raisins.

Dust chilled cake pan with flour and pour batter into pan, spread evenly. Bake for 55–60 minutes. Invert cake on a wire rack and allow to cool in the pan for 5 minutes. Remove pan. Cool cake. Slice to serve.

Pound Cake

1 c. butter, softened
1 1/4 c. sugar
4 eggs
1/2 c. brewed coffee
2 tsp. vanilla extract
2 1/4 c. flour
1 tsp. baking powder
1/2 tsp. salt
1/2 tsp. mace

Preheat oven to 325°F.

Cream butter and sugar until light and fluffy. Add eggs, one at a time, beating well after each addition.

Stir in coffee and vanilla extract.

In a separate bowl, sift together dry ingredients; add to the creamed mixture.

Pour into a well-greased 9 x 5-inch loaf pan, the bottom of which has been lined with parchment paper.

Bake for 1 1/4 hours, or until cake tests done.

Cool in pan for 15 minutes.

Turn out on a wire rack to cool completely.

Classic Chocolate Pound Cake

1 pkg. German sweet chocolate
1/4 c. water
2 sticks butter or margarine
3 c. sugar
6 large eggs
3 c. all-purpose flour
1/2 tsp. baking powder
1/2 tsp. salt
3/4 c. milk
1 tsp. vanilla extract
1/2 tsp. almond extract (optional)

Preheat oven to 325°F. Grease and flour a Bundt pan.

Over low heat, stir chocolate and water until melted. Remove from heat and set aside.

In a large bowl, use an electric mixer to cream the butter and sugar.

Add the eggs, one at a time, creaming well after each addition. Add melted chocolate.

Combine flour, baking powder, and salt in a separate bowl.

Add to the creamed mixture alternately with milk, blending well after each addition. Stir in vanilla and almond extracts.

Bake for 1 1/4 hours. Cool in the pan for 20 minutes. Slide a blunt knife or spatula around the edge of the cake to loosen the sides.

Cool another 30 minutes before removing the pan. Invert on a serving platter. Dust with confectioners' sugar.

Makes 12 servings.

Cream Cheese Carrot Cake

2 c. flour
1 3/4 c. sugar
1 1/4 tsp. baking soda
1 tsp. salt
2 tsp. cinnamon
3/4 c. olive oil
1/2 c. milk
3 large eggs
3 c. finely grated raw carrots
1/2 to 1 c. chopped pecans
Cream Cheese Frosting (recipe follows)

Preheat oven to 350°F. Grease and flour a 9 x 13 x 2-inch pan.

Sift together flour, sugar, soda, salt, and cinnamon. Add oil, milk, and eggs. Blend on low speed for 1 minute. Add carrots and pecans; mix until well blended. Pour into prepared pan. Bake for 40–45 minutes, or until a toothpick inserted in the center comes out clean. When completely cool, frost with Cream Cheese Frosting.

Cream Cheese Frosting:
6 oz. cream cheese, softened
6 tbsp. butter, softened
3/4 tsp. vanilla extract
2 1/4 c. confectioners' sugar
1/3 c. flaked coconut
1/3 c. chopped pecans
1/3 c. raisins

Mix together cream cheese, butter, and vanilla extract. Add confectioners' sugar and beat until light and fluffy. Blend in coconut, pecans, and raisins.

Lemon Poppy Cake

3 c. all-purpose flour
2 c. sugar
1/4 c. poppy seed
1 c. sweet, unsalted butter, softened
1 c. buttermilk
4 eggs
1/2 tsp. baking soda
1/2 tsp. baking powder
1/2 tsp. salt
4 tsp. grated lemon peel
1/2 tsp. vanilla extract

Glaze:
1 c. confectioners' sugar
1–2 tbsp. lemon juice

Preheat oven to 325°F. Grease and lightly flour a 10-inch Bundt pan.

Combine all cake ingredients in a large mixing bowl. Using an electric mixer, beat at low speed until all ingredients are moistened. Then beat at high speed until batter is smooth, about 1–2 minutes. Pour batter into prepared pan. Bake for 55–65 minutes, or until a toothpick inserted in the center comes out clean. Allow to cool for 10 minutes. Remove from pan and cool completely.

In small bowl, stir together confectioners' sugar and lemon juice until smooth. Drizzle over cake and serve.

10

Blueberries and Cream Cake

1/2 c. butter or margarine, softened
1 c. plus 2 tbsp. sugar, divided
2 eggs
1 tbsp. lemon juice
1 tsp. grated lemon peel
2 c. all-purpose flour
2 tsp. baking powder
1/2 tsp. salt
1/2 c. milk
1 c. blueberries, divided

Cream:
1 c. whipping cream
2 tbsp. sugar
2 tbsp. lemon or orange liqueur

Preheat oven to 375°F. Grease a 9-inch springform pan. Line the bottom with wax paper, then grease and flour the paper.

Beat butter and 1 cup sugar until light and fluffy. Add eggs, one at a time, blending well after each addition. Beat in lemon juice and peel.

In a separate bowl, combine flour, baking powder, and salt. Gradually add to butter mixture alternately with milk.

Chop half of the blueberries and add to the batter. Pour batter into pan. Sprinkle remaining blueberries on top and dust with 2 tablespoons sugar. Bake for 40 minutes. Remove from oven and cool for 10 minutes in the pan. Remove sides of pan. Serve warm with dollops of cream.

Prepare cream while cake is baking. Using chilled beaters, beat whipping cream and 2 tablespoons sugar in a chilled mixing bowl, until stiff. Beat in liqueur.

Pineapple Upside-Down Cake

1 tbsp. butter, softened
1/2 c. light brown sugar, packed
3 cans (8 oz. each) pineapple slices in unsweetened juice
9 maraschino cherries
1 c. cake flour
3/4 c. sugar
1 1/2 tsp. baking powder
1/4 c. frozen egg substitute (equivalent to 1 egg), thawed
1/2 tsp. vanilla extract
1/4 tsp. coconut extract

Preheat oven to 350°F. Butter a 9 x 9-inch baking pan. Sprinkle brown sugar over the bottom of the pan. Drain the pineapple slices, reserving 1/2 cup of juice. Place 9 pineapple slices on top of the brown sugar in the pan. Place 1 cherry in the center of each pineapple slice.

Purée 2 pineapple slices; set aside. Stir together cake flour, sugar, and baking powder; set aside.

In a separate bowl, combine puréed pineapple, pineapple juice, egg substitute, vanilla extract, and coconut extract. Add to dry ingredients, stirring until just blended. Pour into the prepared pan, spreading evenly. Bake for 20–25 minutes, or until a toothpick inserted in the center comes out clean. Allow to cool for 5 minutes. Using a blunt knife or a spatula, loosen cake from edges of pan. Invert a serving platter on top of the baking pan. Flip the pan along with the platter over. Shake gently to remove the pan. Slice cake into squares. Serve immediately.

Makes 9 servings.

Royal Cake

1 c. chopped dates
1 c. boiling water
1 tsp. baking soda
1/4 c. butter, softened
1 c. sugar
1 tsp. vanilla extract
1 1/2 c. cake flour
1 tsp. baking powder
1/4 tsp. salt
1/2 c. chopped walnuts (optional)

Topping:
4 tsp. butter
1/2 c. brown sugar
3 tsp. whipping cream
1/2 c. sweetened flaked coconut

Preheat oven to 350°F. Lightly grease an 8 x 8-inch baking pan.

Mix together dates, boiling water, and soda until well blended; set aside.

In a large mixing bowl, cream the butter and sugar until they are light and fluffy. Stir in vanilla extract; set aside.

In a separate bowl, sift together flour, baking powder, and salt. Alternately add the flour mixture and date mixture to the butter mixture. Stir in walnuts. Pour batter into the prepared pan. Bake for 30 minutes.

While cake is baking, prepare the topping by melting the butter, brown sugar, and whipping cream in a saucepan. Bring to a boil, stirring constantly. Remove from heat and stir in coconut. Spread over warm cake. Preheat broiler and broil cake until topping is bubbly, checking constantly to prevent burning. When cake is cool, cut into squares and serve.

Makes 12 servings.

Gumdrop Cake

1 c. brown sugar
1 c. granulated sugar
2 c. shortening
4 eggs
4 tsp. baking soda, divided
2 c. applesauce
4 c. sifted flour
1 c. dates
1 c. walnuts
1 c. raisins
1 c. small mixed gumdrops
1 tsp. salt
2 tsp. cinnamon
2 tsp. nutmeg
2 tsp. allspice

Blend sugars with shortening. Add eggs, mixing well.

Dissolve 2 teaspoons baking soda in the applesauce.

In a separate bowl, mix flour, dates, walnuts, raisins, gumdrops, and salt. Add applesauce and mix. Blend all into sugar mixture. Add spices and remaining baking soda; blend. Pour into two greased loaf pans. Bake at 325° for 1 hour, or until done.

Bourbon Cake

3/4 lb. butter
2 c. granulated sugar, divided
2 1/4 c. light brown sugar, firmly packed, divided
6 eggs
5 1/2 c. all-purpose flour
1/4 tsp. salt
1 tsp. mace
2 c. bourbon whiskey
3 1/2 c. (1 lb.) pecans, chopped

Cream together butter, 1 cup granulated sugar, and 1 1/8 cups brown sugar.

In a separate bowl, beat the eggs with the remaining 1 cup granulated sugar and 1 1/8 cups brown sugar until light and fluffy. Add to butter mixture and blend.

Sift together the flour, salt, and mace. Add the flour mixture to the butter mixture a little at a time, alternating with the whiskey. Lastly, stir pecans into the batter. Bake in a slow oven in a 10-inch Bundt pan for 2 to 2 1/2 hours, or until a knife inserted into the cake comes out clean. Allow cake to cool. Remove from pan and wrap in aluminum foil. Allow cake to set in the refrigerator for 1 week to allow flavors to "season."

Rum Cake

1/2 c. plus 2 tbsp. plain flour
2 tbsp. cocoa
1 level tsp. baking powder
1/2 c. plus 2 tbsp. soft brown sugar
2 eggs, separated
6 tbsp. salad oil
8 tbsp. milk, divided
1 tsp. vanilla extract
4 tbsp. rum
1/4 pt. cream
2 level tbsp. confectioners' sugar, sifted
10 walnut halves

Preheat oven to 350°F. Line and generously grease an 8-inch square baking pan.

Sift flour, cocoa, and baking powder into a bowl; stir in brown sugar. Add egg yolks, oil, 6 tablespoons milk, and vanilla extract; beat until batter is smooth.

In a separate bowl, beat egg whites until soft peaks form. Fold the egg whites into the batter with a large metal spoon. Pour batter into the prepared pan and bake for 1 1/4 hours, or until golden and a toothpick inserted in the center comes out clean.

Remove from oven and allow to cool in the pan for 10 minutes. Turn out on a wire rack. Using a skewer, poke several holes in the cake.

Pour rum over the cake. Allow to set until cake is completely cooled.

Beat cream, remaining milk, and confectioners' sugar until thick.

Spoon on top of cake and garnish with walnut halves.

Apricot Almond Cream Cake

1 can (16 oz.) apricot halves in light syrup
2 c. cake flour
1 tsp. baking powder
1 tsp. baking soda
1/4 tsp. salt
4 oz. unsalted butter, softened
1 c. sugar
2 eggs
1/2 tsp. vanilla extract
1/4 tsp. almond extract
1 c. sour cream
1/4 c. sliced almonds

Grease a 9-inch cake pan and line with greased baking parchment or wax paper. Preheat the oven to 350°F. Drain the apricots and discard the liquid. Cut each half in half. Set aside. Whisk together the flour, baking powder, baking soda, and salt. Set aside.

In a large bowl, with an electric mixer, cream together the butter and sugar for 3–4 minutes, or until the mixture is light in color and fluffy.

Add the eggs, one at a time, beating until thoroughly mixed. Scrape down the bowl, add the vanilla and almond extracts, and mix until combined.

On low speed, add, in order, one-third of flour mixture, half of the sour cream, half the remaining flour mixture, then the remaining sour cream and the remaining flour, mixing just to combine after each addition and scraping down the sides of the bowl.

Pour the batter into the prepared pan and level it with a spatula. Arrange the apricot quarters in a decorative pattern on top of the batter. Sprinkle the sliced almonds over any exposed batter. Bake for 45–50 minutes, or until a cake tester inserted near the center comes out clean. Let the cake cool in the pan for 10 minutes. Turn the cake out on a plate, remove the parchment or wax paper liner from the bottom, and then flip the cake on a cooling rack.

Moist Blueberry Cake

2 c. blueberries
2 tbsp. lemon juice
1 c. flour
2 tsp. baking powder
1/4 tsp. salt
1/2 tsp. nutmeg
3/4 c. sugar
1/2 c. milk
1 egg
1/4 c. butter, melted
1 tsp. vanilla extract
1 c. sugar
1 tbsp. cornstarch
1 c. boiling water

Place blueberries and lemon juice in an 8 x 8-inch pan. Mix flour, baking powder, salt, nutmeg, and 3/4 cup sugar. Beat in milk, egg, melted butter, and vanilla. Spread over berries.

Mix 1 cup sugar with cornstarch and sprinkle over batter. Pour boiling water over all.

Bake at 350° for 40–50 minutes.

Strawberries

Blend:
To thoroughly mix two or more ingredients.

Boil:
To raise the temperature of a liquid until it bubbles; The boiling temperature of water is 212° F (or 100° C).

Strawberry Pie

1/2 to 1 c. sugar, to taste
1/4 c. all-purpose flour
1/8 tsp. salt
4 c. strawberries, washed and hulled
2 tbsp. butter
pastry for single crust pie
whipped cream

Preheat oven to 425°F.

Combine sugar, flour, and salt. Add strawberries and toss lightly. Pour fruit mixture into a 1-quart baking dish. Dot with butter.

Roll pie pastry out to a size that is 1 inch larger than the top of the baking dish. Wrap pastry around a rolling pin and transfer to top of baking dish. Fold pastry edges under and press firmly to dish rim. Flute edges. Make several small slashes in the pastry for steam vents. Bake for 25 minutes, or until crust is browned. Serve slightly warm with whipped cream.

Makes 6 servings.

Berry Bliss

1 pkg. (6 oz.) strawberry-flavored gelatin
1 c. boiling water
2 pkgs. (10 oz. each) frozen sliced strawberries in syrup, thawed
1 can (20 oz.) crushed pineapple, drained
3 medium bananas, sliced
1 c. coarsely chopped walnuts
2 c. sour cream

In a large bowl, mix gelatin and boiling water until gelatin is dissolved. Chill until partially set.

Stir in strawberries, pineapple, bananas, and walnuts. Turn half of the mixture into a 13 x 9 x 2-inch dish. Freeze for 10–12 minutes, or until firm.

When firm, spread with sour cream. Spoon remaining strawberry mixture over sour cream. Cover and chill for at least 4 hours, or until firm.

Makes 24 servings.

Strawberries with Yogurt Sauce

1 c. double-thick yogurt
1/4 c. brown sugar, firmly packed
1/2 tsp. ground cinnamon
1 tsp. vanilla extract
2 tbsp. strawberry liqueur (optional)
2 pt. (24 oz.) fresh strawberries, washed, hulled, and cut into bite-size pieces
2 tbsp. pecan pieces, lightly toasted

In a mixing bowl, whisk together yogurt, brown sugar, cinnamon, vanilla extract, and strawberry liqueur until well mixed. Refrigerate for 1 hour, or until slightly firm.

Spoon strawberry pieces into 4 individual serving dishes. Top each with 1/4 cup of sauce. Garnish with nuts. Serve immediately.

Makes 4 servings.

Strawberries and Cream Celebration

2 1/2 c. cake flour, sifted
1 2/3 c. sugar
4 tsp. baking powder
1 tsp. salt
1/2 c. butter
1 1/4 c. milk, divided
1 tsp. lemon extract
1/2 tsp. vanilla extract
5 egg yolks
4 c. strawberries
2 c. heavy cream, whipped with 1/4 c. sugar and 1 tsp. vanilla extract, divided
3/4 c. red current jelly

Preheat oven to 350°F. Line 2 cake pans with parchment paper and butter generously; set aside.

In a large mixing bowl, sift together the cake flour, 1 2/3 cups sugar, baking powder, and salt.

Add butter and half of the milk. Using an electric mixer, beat at medium speed for 2 minutes. Add remaining milk, lemon extract, 1/2 teaspoon vanilla extract, and egg yolks. Beat for an additional 2 minutes.

Pour batter into prepared pans. Bake for 30 minutes, or until a toothpick inserted in the center comes out clean. Remove from oven and allow to cool.

Wash and hull strawberries. Chop enough strawberries to make 1 cup, set aside the remaining berries. Fold the chopped strawberries into 1 cup of the whipped cream mixture.

Place one cake layer on a serving plate and spread the top with the strawberry-cream filling. Place the second cake layer on top.

Slice the reserved strawberries lengthwise and arrange them in circles on top of the cake so that the pointed ends are toward the edge of the cake.

Refrigerate cake for 10 minutes.

In a small saucepan over low heat, melt the red currant jelly, stirring constantly. Carefully brush the hot jelly over the strawberries. Spread some of the whipped cream around the sides of the cake.

Spoon remaining whipped cream into a pastry bag fitted with a rosette tip. Pipe rosettes between the strawberry points around the rim of the cake.

Change to a star tube and connect the rosettes. Using a leaf tip, pipe a border around the bottom edge of the cake. Refrigerate until ready to serve.

Strawberry Candy

1 large pkg. strawberry-flavored gelatin
1 lb. flaked coconut
1 can Eagle Brand milk
red colored sugar
green colored sugar
green toothpicks

In an airtight container, stir gelatin, coconut, and milk together, mixing thoroughly. Place in the refrigerator for 3–4 days. Form into strawberry shapes. Roll in red sugar. Dip top in green sugar for the "leaves." Place 1/2 a green toothpick in the top of each for the "stem."

Strawberry Buttercream Cake

2 1/2 c. cake flour
1 1/2 c. sugar
2 tsp. baking powder
1 tsp. salt
1 1/4 c. whipping cream
4 eggs
1 1/2 tsp. vanilla extract
Strawberry Buttercream Frosting (recipe follows)
fresh strawberries, for garnish

Preheat oven to 350°F. Grease and lightly flour two 9-inch round cake pans.

Combine flour, sugar, baking powder, and salt.

In a medium bowl, beat whipping cream until stiff; set aside.

Beat eggs in a small bowl until they are thick and light. Add vanilla extract, beating well. Fold eggs into whipped cream.

Sift flour mixture over cream mixture; gently fold into batter until smooth. Pour into prepared pans. Bake for 30 minutes, or until center springs back when lightly touched. Cool in pans on wire racks for 10 minutes. Gently loosen sides with a blunt knife or spatula. Invert on wire racks and allow to cool completely. Spread Strawberry Buttercream Frosting between the layers. Then frost tops and sides of cake. Garnish with fresh strawberries.

Strawberry Buttercream Frosting:
1 pt. strawberries
1/2 c. butter, softened
1 lb. confectioners' sugar

Mash enough strawberries to equal 1/2 cup. In a medium bowl, cream butter. Mix in mashed strawberries. Slowly add confectioners' sugar, mixing until smooth.

Strawberry Dessert Topping

20 oz. frozen strawberries
2 tsp. lemon juice
1/4 c. sugar

In a colander placed atop a large bowl, thaw the strawberries. Press to squeeze out the juice. You will need to get about 1 1/4 cups of juice; this will take several hours.

Place juice in a microwave-safe dish and microwave until juice is reduced to 1/4 cup.

Purée strawberries. Add reduced juice, lemon juice, and sugar. Serve over favorite cake, torte, or ice cream.

Makes 1 1/3 cups of topping.

Apples

Combine:
To stir together two or more ingredients.

Cream:
To beat a mixture with a spoon or electric mixer until it is smooth, light, fluffy, and nearly twice its original volume.

Apple Pie

Pie:
1/2 c. sugar
1/4 c. flour
1 tsp. ground cinnamon
dash of salt
8 cups thinly sliced and pared tart apples
   (6–8 apples)
1 (9-inch) pie crust

Crumb Topping:
3/4 c. flour
1/2 c. sugar
1/3 c. butter or margarine
1 tsp. cinnamon
1 tsp. nutmeg
pinch of cloves
pinch of mace

Preheat oven to 450°F.

For filling, mix sugar, flour, cinnamon, and salt in a large bowl. Stir in apples. Turn mixture into the pie crust, pressing apples down firmly.

For crumb topping, combine flour and sugar in a medium bowl. Using a knife or pastry blender, cut in butter until mixture resembles a coarse meal. Add spices. Sprinkle the crumb mixture on top of the pie, pressing the crumbs into the apples.

Bake for 10 minutes. Lower temperature to 350°F and bake for an additional 40 minutes, or until done.

Apple Crumbles

8–10 apples, peeled, cored, and sliced
1 c. sugar
ground cinnamon
1 stick butter, softened
1 c. brown sugar
pinch of salt
1 c. flour

Spread apples in the bottom of a rectangular baking pan. Apples should reach almost to the top of the pan. Pour sugar evenly over the apples. Sprinkle with cinnamon to taste. In a bowl, mix butter, brown sugar, salt, and flour until it resembles a coarse meal. Spread over apples. Bake at 350°F for 30 minutes, or until the apples are tender. Serve warm or cold. Top with vanilla ice cream, if desired.

Apple Roll

2 tbsp. sugar plus 1 3/4 c. sugar, divided
2 c. flour
pinch of salt
2 tbsp. shortening
1/2 c. milk
2 tsp. baking powder
1 c. apples, chopped
2 tbsp. butter, melted
1/4 c. cinnamon

Mix together 2 tablespoons sugar, flour, salt, shortening, milk, and baking powder. Roll dough to 1 inch thick; spread with apples. Roll up dough and cut into 1 1/2-inch slices. Combine 1 1/2 cups sugar and 2 cups water in a pan and heat to boiling. Place rolls in baking pan with hot syrup. Sprinkle with remaining sugar, cinnamon, and butter. Bake in moderate oven until brown.

Old World Apple Tart

Pastry:
1 1/2 c. all-purpose flour
1/2 c. sugar
1/2 c. butter or margarine, softened
1 egg
1/4 tsp. almond extract

Filling:
1/2 c. golden or dark raisins
1/3 c. sliced almonds
2 large Granny Smith apples, peeled, cored, and cut into 1/4-inch slices
2 tsp. cornstarch
1/4 c. low-fat milk
3 tsp. lemon juice
1/4 tsp. almond extract
1/4 tsp. vanilla extract
8 oz. vanilla yogurt
1 egg, beaten
1/4 c. apricot preserves, melted
whipped topping (optional)

Preheat oven to 375°F.

For pastry, combine flour, sugar, and butter in a large bowl. Beat at low speed until well mixed. Beat in 1 egg and 1/4 teaspoon almond extract until mixture is crumbly. Press mixture into the bottom of a 9-inch springform pan, pressing crust 1 1/2 inches up the sides. Sprinkle raisins and almonds over pastry. Arrange apple slices over raisins and almonds in desired pattern.

In a medium bowl, dissolve cornstarch in milk. Add lemon juice, 1/4 teaspoon almond extract, vanilla extract, yogurt, and beaten egg; blend well. Pour over apples.

Bake for 55–65 minutes, or until the apples are tender. Allow to cool for 30 minutes. Remove sides of pan. Brush the apricot preserves over the apples. Garnish with whipped topping, if desired. Store in refrigerator.

Makes 12 servings.

Apple Raisin Squares

1 1/2 c. flour
1/2 tsp. salt
1/2 tsp. soda
1 1/2 c. uncooked rolled oats
1 c. brown sugar
1/2 c. butter or margarine, melted
2 eggs
2 c. chopped apples
1 tbsp. lemon juice
1/3 c. raisins
1/3 c. chopped nuts
confectioners' sugar

Preheat oven to 375°F.

Combine flour, salt, and soda. Mix in oats and brown sugar. Gradually add melted butter and eggs, stirring with a fork until mixture is crumbly. Firmly press half of mixture into a greased 9-inch square baking pan.

Stir together apples and lemon juice. Mix in raisins and nuts. Evenly spread apple mixture over the crumb base. Roll remaining crumb mixture between 2 sheets of wax paper to form a 9-inch square. Remove top sheet of wax paper and invert the dough over the filling, pressing the dough down lightly. Remove wax paper. Bake for 30 minutes. Dust with confectioners' sugar.

Apple Cranberry Pie

1 (15-oz.) pkg. refrigerated pie crust

Filling:
4 c. sliced and peeled sweet cooking apples (e.g., Golden Delicious)
2 c. fresh or frozen cranberries
1/2 c. sugar
1/4 c. flour
1/4 c. brown sugar, firmly packed
1/2 tsp. cinnamon
1/4 tsp. nutmeg

Topping:
1/2 c. all-purpose flour
1/3 c. brown sugar, firmly packed
1/4 tsp. cinnamon
dash nutmeg
1/4 c. butter or margarine
1/3 c. chopped pecans

Preheat oven to 375°F. Prepare the pie crust as package directs for a one-crust filled pie using a 9-inch pie pan.

Combine apples and cranberries in a large bowl.

In a separate bowl, combine remaining filling ingredients, and mix well.

Add to fruit mixture, tossing to coat. Pour into crust.

Combine all topping ingredients, except butter and pecans, in a small bowl. Using a knife or pastry blender, cut in butter until crumbly. Stir in pecans. Sprinkle evenly over the top of the pie.

Bake for 45–55 minutes, or until the apples are tender and the crust and topping are golden brown.

To prevent excessive browning, cover crust edges with strips of foil after 15–20 minutes of baking. Serve warm with whipped cream or ice cream, if desired.

Makes 8 servings.

Baked Apples

4 apples
4 tbsp. brown sugar, divided
2 tbsp. butter or margarine, divided

Core each apple, being careful to leave some apple at the bottom of each.

Place 1 tablespoon of brown sugar, 1/2 tablespoon of butter, and a sprinkle of cinnamon in the center of each apple.

Place apples in a microwave-safe dish. Cook on high in the microwave for 4 to 6 1/2 minutes. Serve warm.

Makes 4 servings.

Cobblers & Fruits

Cut In:
To mix a solid fat, such as butter, with dry ingredients using a pastry cutter, food processor, or two knives.

Dough:
A thick mixture of flour and liquid that is combined with other ingredients to make recipes such as cookies or bread.

Basic Fruit Cobbler

1 3/4 c. sugar, divided
1 c. flour
2 tsp. baking powder
3/4 c. milk
1/2 c. butter or margarine, melted
3 c. favorite fruit

Preheat oven to 350°F. In a bowl, combine 1 cup sugar, flour, baking powder, and milk.

Pour melted butter in the bottom of a 6 x 9-inch baking pan. Pour sugar mixture over butter; do not mix. Place favorite fruit over mixture; do not mix. Sprinkle remaining 3/4 cup of sugar over fruit. Bake for 1 hour. Serve warm.

Peach Cobbler

1 1/4 c. flour, divided
1 c. granulated sugar, divided
1/2 c. light brown sugar
1/4 tsp. salt
1/2 tsp. cinnamon
1/2 c. butter or margarine
4 c. sliced fresh peaches
1 tbsp. lemon juice
1 tsp. lemon peel

Combine 1 cup flour, 1/2 cup granulated sugar, brown sugar, salt, and cinnamon. Cut in butter with 2 knives until mixture resembles coarse cornmeal.

In a separate bowl, combine peaches, lemon juice, lemon peel, 1/2 cup sugar, and 1/4 cup flour. Spoon into a greased 9-inch square dish. Sprinkle flour mixture over peaches. Bake at 350°F, covered, for 15 minutes. Remove cover and bake 35–45 minutes longer.

Cherry Surprise

1 1/2 c. flour
1 tsp. salt
1/2 tsp. baking soda
1 c. brown sugar, firmly packed
3/4 c. quick cooking oatmeal
1/2 c. shortening
2 cans cherry pie filling
whipped topping or ice cream

Sift together flour, salt, and baking soda. Add brown sugar and oatmeal; mix. Cut in shortening until crumbs the size of small peas form. Press half of mixture into an ungreased 9 x 13-inch pan. Cover with pie filling. Spread remaining oatmeal mixture over this. Press down gently with the back of a spoon. Bake at 350°F for 25–30 minutes. Serve warm with whipped topping or ice cream.

Creamy Orange Fruit Dip

2 large oranges
1 pkg. (8 oz.) whipped cream cheese
1/3 c. confectioners' sugar
1/4 c. milk
1 1/2 tsp. orange extract

Grate peel from oranges. Wrap half of orange peel with plastic wrap and refrigerate. Reserve oranges. In a small bowl, combine cream cheese, sugar, milk, and extract, beating until smooth. Stir in remaining grated orange peel. Cover and refrigerate until ready to serve.

To serve, place dip in a decorative bowl, and garnish with reserved grated orange peel. Serve with orange sections, strawberries, pineapple chunks, grapes, kiwi fruit, cantaloupe, honeydew, or watermelon chunks.

Apples and Prunes Cobbler

2 lb. firm cooking apples
1 c. pitted prunes (about 8 oz.)
1/2 c. walnut pieces, coarsely chopped
1/2 c. plus 1 tbsp. sugar, divided
1/2 tsp. cinnamon
2 tbsp. all-purpose flour
2 tbsp. fresh lemon juice
butter
Buttermilk Dough (recipe follows)
1 tbsp. milk or buttermilk

Preheat oven to 375°F.

Peel, halve, and core the apples. Slice each half into 5–6 wedges. Slice each prune into 3–4 strips. In a large bowl, combine the apples, prunes, and chopped walnuts.

In a bowl, combine 1/2 cup sugar, cinnamon, and flour. Toss with the fruit and nut mixture. Pour into a 1 1/2-quart, shallow baking dish. Sprinkle top with lemon juice and dot with butter.

On a lightly floured surface, roll out the Buttermilk Dough to a size slightly larger than the baking dish. Dough should be about 1/4 inch thick. Place dough on top of the filling and trim off any overhang. Flute the edge of the dough. Slash 4–5 one-inch vent holes in the center of the crust. Brush the dough with milk and sprinkle with the remaining 1 tablespoon of sugar.

Bake the cobbler for 30 minutes, or until the dough is golden and baked through, and the filling is beginning to bubble. Cool on a rack. Serve warm or at room temperature.

Buttermilk Dough:
3/4 c. all-purpose flour
3/4 c. cake flour
1 1/2 tsp. baking powder
1/2 tsp. salt
4 tbsp. cold butter
3/4 c. buttermilk or milk

Combine flours, baking powder, and salt. Sift into a mixing bowl.

Cut the butter into 8–10 pieces, then add it to the dry ingredients. Rub the butter with your fingertips until the mixture resembles coarse meal. Make a well in the center of the mixture and add the buttermilk. Toss with a fork to moisten evenly. Let the dough stand for 1 minute to absorb the liquid. Turn out on a floured surface. Knead dough 2–3 times, or until it is smooth and less sticky.

Nutty Bananas

chopped peanuts
milk chocolate pieces or
   semi-sweet chocolate pieces
bananas

Cover a plate with wax paper. Place chopped peanuts in a bowl.

In the top of a double boiler, melt chocolate over hot water. Stir constantly until chocolate is melted and smooth. Remove from heat.

Remove banana skin and cut banana in half crossways. Skewer each half on a wooden stick, such as an ice cream stick. Dip in chocolate, rolling until all sides are coated. Roll in peanuts. Place on wax paper. Freeze until hard. Wrap in plastic wrap and freeze until ready to serve.

Pineapple Bake

3–4 c. bread crumbs, no crusts
3/4 c. butter or margarine, melted
1 1/2 c. sugar
1 can (20 oz.) crushed pineapple, undrained
3 eggs, beaten
2–3 tbsp. milk

Combine all ingredients, except milk, stirring to mix. Pour into a lightly greased 9 x 13-inch baking pan. Drizzle milk over top to brown. Bake at 350°F for 45 minutes.

Pineapple Banana Treat

1 1/2 c. graham cracker crumbs
1/4 c. sugar
1/3 c. butter or margarine, melted
3 bananas, sliced
1 pkg. (8 oz.) cream cheese, softened
3 1/2 c. cold milk
2 pkgs. (4 oz. each) instant vanilla pudding
1 can (20 oz.) crushed pineapple, drained
1 tub (8 oz.) whipped topping, thawed

To form the crust, mix graham cracker crumbs, sugar, and butter. Press evenly into the bottom of a 13 x 9 x 2-inch baking dish. Arrange banana slices on top of the crust.

Using a wire whisk, beat the cream cheese until it is smooth. Gradually add milk, beating well. Add pudding mixes and beat until thick and well blended. Spread evenly over banana slices. Layer pineapple evenly over pudding mixture. Cover all with whipped topping. Refrigerate 3 hours, or until ready to serve.

Makes 15 servings.

Fried Bananas

4 large bananas
2 tbsp. sugar
2 tbsp. lemon juice
1/2 tsp. grated orange peel
3 oz. rum
2 tbsp. flour
1/2 c. water
1 tbsp. olive oil
1 egg white, beaten stiff
1/2 c. olive oil
sugar

Cut bananas in half lengthwise. Place in a casserole dish. Sprinkle with sugar, lemon juice, orange peel, and rum. Let stand 2 hours.

Mix together flour, water, and 1 tablespoon of olive oil; blending well. Gently stir in beaten egg white.

Heat 1/2 cup of olive oil in a deep fryer. Drain bananas, dip into batter, and fry until just golden. Sprinkle with sugar and serve hot.

Bananas Foster

1 tbsp. butter
2 tbsp. brown sugar
1 ripe banana, peeled and
    sliced lengthwise
1/8 tsp. cinnamon
1/2 oz. banana liqueur
1 oz. white rum

Melt butter in a chafing dish. Add brown sugar and blend well. Add banana and saute. Sprinkle with cinnamon. Pour over banana liqueur and rum and ignite, basting banana with flaming liquid. Serve when flame dies out.

Pies

Dredge:
To coat, usually with flour.

Drizzle:
To pour a liquid, such as butter, over food in a thin stream.

Dust:
To lightly sprinkle an ingredient, such as confectioners' sugar, over a food.

Pecan Pie

3 eggs
2/3 c. sugar
1/2 tsp. salt
1/3 c. butter, melted
1 c. light corn syrup
1 c. pecan halves or crushed pecans
1 (9-inch) pie crust, baked

Beat eggs, sugar, salt, butter, and syrup with an electric mixer. Stir in pecans. Pour into baked pie crust. Bake at 375°F for 40–50 minutes, or until the center is set. To prevent crust edges from burning, cover edges with strips of aluminum foil before baking. Remove foil for the last 5–10 minutes of baking so that edges will brown slightly.

Turtle Pie

3/4 c. finely crushed chocolate wafer cookies
4 c. frozen nonfat vanilla yogurt, softened, divided
1/3 c. chopped pecans, divided
1/3 c. nonfat caramel ice cream topping, divided
1/4 c. chocolate-flavored syrup, divided

Coat a 9-inch pie pan with nonstick cooking spray. Add cookie crumbs, tilting pan to coat evenly. (Avoid tapping pan as this will loosen crumbs from sides.) Gently press crumbs against sides and bottom of pan.

In medium bowl, use an electric mixer to beat frozen yogurt just until smooth. Spoon half of the yogurt into small mounds in the coated pie pan. Gently spread mounds in an even layer, being careful not to pull crumbs away from pan.

Sprinkle 1/4 cup pecans over the yogurt. Drizzle with 1/4 cup caramel topping and 3 tablespoons chocolate syrup. Add remaining yogurt, spreading gently. Sprinkle with remaining pecans, and drizzle with remaining caramel topping and chocolate syrup. Freeze 2–4 hours, or until firm.

Makes 8 servings.

Fudge Pie

1/4 c. butter or margarine
3/4 c. brown sugar, firmly packed
3 large eggs
12 oz. chocolate chips, melted and cooled
2 tsp. instant coffee powder
1 tsp. rum extract
1/4 c. unbleached flour
1 c. walnuts, coarsely chopped
1 (9-inch) pie shell, unbaked
walnut halves

Preheat oven to 375°F.

Using an electric mixer on medium speed, cream together the butter and sugar until light and fluffy. Add eggs, one at a time, beating well after each addition. Add chocolate, coffee powder, and rum extract, blending well. Stir in flour and chopped walnuts.

Turn into the pie shell. Arrange walnut halves around the edge of the pie. Bake for 25 minutes, or until set around the edge. Cool on a wire rack.

Makes 6 servings.

Boston Cream Pie

2 eggs, separated
1/2 c. sugar
2 1/4 c. cake flour, sifted
1 c. sugar
3 tsp. baking powder
1 tsp. salt
1/3 c. salad oil
1 c. milk, divided
1 1/2 tsp. vanilla extract
Cream Filling (recipe follows)
Chocolate Glaze (recipe follows)

Beat egg whites until soft peaks form. Gradually add 1/2 cup sugar, beating until very stiff peaks form; set aside.

In a separate bowl, sift together flour, 1 cup sugar, baking powder, and salt. Add oil, 1/2 cup milk, and vanilla extract. Using an electric mixer, beat at medium speed for 1 minute. Add remaining milk and egg yolks. Beat for 1 minute and scrape the bowl. Gently fold in the egg white mixture.

Pour mixture into 2 greased and lightly floured, 9-inch cake pans. Bake at 350°F for 20 minutes, or until done. Remove from oven and allow to cool for 10 minutes. Remove from pans and cool completely.

Spread Cream Filling between layers and frost with Chocolate Glaze.

Cream Filling:
1/3 c. sugar
3 tbsp. flour
1/4 tsp. salt
1 1/4 c. milk
1 egg, beaten
1 tbsp. butter
1 tsp. vanilla extract

Combine sugar, flour, and salt in a saucepan. Gradually add milk, mixing well. Cook over medium heat, stirring constantly until mixture boils and thickens. Cook and stir for 2 minutes more. Slowly add the hot mixture into the beaten egg, and then return all to the saucepan. Cook and stir until mixture begins to boil again. Stir in butter and vanilla extract. Cover with wax paper and cool.

Chocolate Glaze:
1 1/2 (1-oz.) squares unsweetened chocolate
2 tbsp. butter
1 1/2 c. confectioners' sugar, sifted
1 tsp. vanilla extract
3 tbsp. boiling water
2–3 tsp. water

Melt chocolate and butter over low heat, stirring constantly. Remove from heat, and stir in confectioners' sugar and vanilla extract until crumbly. Stir in 3 tablespoons boiling water. Add additional water 1 teaspoon at a time to form a glaze of pouring consistency. Pour quickly over the cake and spread evenly over the top and sides.

Lemon Chess Pie

1 (15-oz.) pkg. refrigerated pie crust
1/3 c. butter or margarine, softened
1 c. sugar
3 eggs
2 tbsp. flour
1/4 c. lemon juice
3 tsp. grated lemon peel
1/2 c. milk
1/4 tsp. nutmeg

Preheat oven to 450°F.

Prepare the pie crust as package directs for a one-crust filled pie using a 9-inch pie pan. Bake for 5–8 minutes, or until light brown. Reduce oven temperature to 325°F.

While crust is baking, combine butter, sugar, and eggs in a large bowl. Add flour, lemon juice, lemon peel, and milk; mix well. (Mixture may appear curdled.) Pour into prepared crust. Sprinkle with nutmeg.

Bake at 325°F for 40–45 minutes, or until edges of filling begin to brown and center is almost set. To prevent crust edges from burning, cover with strips of aluminum foil after 15–20 minutes of baking. Cool on a wire rack for 30 minutes. Refrigerate 3–4 hours before serving. Top with whipped cream, if desired.

Makes 8 servings.

Lemon Meringue Pie

1 1/2 c. sugar
3 tbsp. cornstarch
3 tbsp. all-purpose flour
1 1/2 c. hot water
3 egg yolks, slightly beaten
2 tbsp. butter or margarine
1/2 tsp. grated lemon peel
1/3 c. lemon juice
1 (9-inch) pastry shell, baked
Meringue (recipe follows)

Combine sugar, cornstarch, and flour in a saucepan. Gradually add the hot water, stirring constantly. Cook over high heat, stirring constantly, until mixtures comes to a boil. Reduce heat and continue to cook and stir for 2 minutes more. Remove from heat.

Stir a small amount of the hot mixture into the egg yolks, then pour all of the egg yolk mixture into the hot mixture. Return mixture to a boil and cook for 2 minutes, stirring constantly. Add butter and lemon peel. Slowly add lemon juice, mixing well. Pour into pastry shell. Spread meringue over filling, sealing the edges. Bake at 350°F for 12–15 minutes. Allow to cool before cutting.

Meringue:
3 egg whites
1/2 tsp. vanilla extract
1/4 tsp. cream of tartar
6 tbsp. sugar

Beat egg whites with vanilla extract and cream of tartar until soft peaks form. Gradually add sugar, beating until all sugar is dissolved and stiff, glossy peaks form.

Lime Pie

1 pkg. (4 oz.) instant vanilla pudding
1/2 c. key lime juice
1 tsp. grated lime peel
14 oz. sweetened condensed milk
green food coloring (optional)
1 (6-oz.) graham cracker pie crust
1/2 c. frozen light whipped topping, thawed
lime slices

Combine pudding mix, lime juice, lime peel, and milk in a medium bowl. Beat for 1–2 minutes, or until well blended. Stir in enough food coloring to achieve the desired color. Pour into pie crust. Refrigerate 10–15 minutes before serving. Top with whipped topping, if desired. Garnish with fresh lime slices.

Makes 8 servings.

Banana Cream Pie

1 (9-inch) pastry shell
3/4 c. sugar
1/3 c. all-purpose flour, or 3 tbsp. cornstarch
1/4 tsp. salt
2 c. milk
3 egg yolks, slightly beaten
2 tbsp. butter
1 tsp. vanilla extract
3–4 bananas
whipped cream (optional)

Bake pastry shell according to package directions. Set aside and allow to cool.

In a saucepan, mix sugar, flour, and salt. Gradually add milk. Cook over medium heat, stirring constantly, until mixture is bubbly. Cook and stir an additional 2 minutes, then remove from heat.

Stir a small amount of hot mixture into egg yolks, then immediately add the entire egg yolk mixture to the hot mixture and cook for 2 minutes, stirring constantly. Remove from heat. Add butter and vanilla extract, stirring until smooth.

Slice 3–4 bananas into the cooled, baked pastry shell. Pour pudding mixture over bananas. Bake at 350°F for 12–15 minutes. Allow to cool. Top with whipped cream, if desired, and serve.

Rocky Road Pie

1 1/2 c. Half-and-Half
1 small pkg. chocolate pudding mix
8 oz. whipped topping
1/3 c. semi-sweet chocolate chips
1/2 c. miniature marshmallows
1/3 c. chopped pecans
1 graham cracker pie crust

Pour half-and-half into large bowl. Add pudding mix. Beat with wire whisk until well blended, about 1 minute. Let stand 5 minutes. Fold in whipped topping, chocolate chips, marshmallows, and nuts. Spoon into pie crust. Freeze until firm, about 6 hours or overnight.

Remove from freezer and let stand 10 minutes to soften before serving. Store leftover pie in freezer.

Raspberry Peach Melba Pie

2 lb. peaches, peeled
1 c. raspberries
2/3 c. brown sugar
3 tbsp. all-purpose flour
1/8 tsp. cinnamon
pinch nutmeg
pastry for 9-inch double crust pie
2 tbsp. butter
1 egg
1 tsp. milk

Preheat oven to 425°F.

Slice peaches into 1/2-inch thick wedges. Place in a large bowl with raspberries.

In a separate bowl, combine sugar, flour, cinnamon, and nutmeg. Add to the fruit mixture and stir to blend; set aside.

Roll out half of the pie pastry and place it in the bottom of a 9-inch pie plate, being careful not to stretch the dough. Do not trim the edges or prick the bottom of the crust. Roll out the remaining dough to form a 10-inch circle that is 1/8 inch thick.

Pour filling into the pie shell and dot with butter. Brush the edge of the pastry with water. Place the remaining pastry circle over the filling. Gently press the seams together to seal. Trim dough to 1/2 inch beyond the edge of the pie plate. Turn the edge under and flute the rim. Cut 2–3 slashes in the top for steam vents.

Whisk together the egg and milk. Brush evenly over the pie crust. Place pie on the bottom oven rack and bake for 10–12 minutes, or until pastry begins to turn golden. Reduce oven heat to 350°F and bake for an additional 45–50 minutes, or until peaches are easily pierced with a fork.

Makes 10 servings.

German Chocolate Pie

3 c. sugar
7 tbsp. baking cocoa
13 oz. evaporated milk
4 large eggs, beaten
1/2 c. butter or margarine, melted
1 tsp. vanilla extract
2 c. flaked coconut
1 c. pecans, chopped
2 (9-inch) pie shells, unbaked

Preheat oven to 350°F.

In a bowl, combine the sugar and cocoa. Add evaporated milk, eggs, melted butter, and vanilla extract, mixing well. Stir in the coconut and pecans.

Turn into the pie shells.

Bake for 40 minutes, or until set around the edges. Cool on wire racks.

Makes 2 pies of 6 servings each.

Raisin Crisscross Pie

1 c. brown sugar, firmly packed
2 tbsp. cornstarch
2 c. raisins
1/2 tsp. finely shredded orange peel
1/2 c. orange juice
1/2 tsp. finely shredded lemon peel
2 tbsp. lemon juice
1 1/3 c. cold water
1/2 c. chopped walnuts
Crisscross Pie Pastry (recipe follows)

Combine brown sugar and cornstarch in a saucepan. Stir in raisins, orange peel, orange juice, lemon peel, lemon juice, and water. Cook over medium heat, stirring constantly, until mixture is thick and bubbly. Continue to cook and stir for 1 minute more. Remove from heat and stir in walnuts. Pour into a pastry-lined, 9-inch pie plate. Arrange crisscross pastry on top; flute the edge. Cover edges of crust with aluminum foil. Bake at 375°F for 20 minutes. Remove foil and bake an additional 20 minutes, or until the crust is golden.

Makes 8 servings.

Crisscross Pie Pastry:
2 c. all-purpose flour
1 tsp. salt
2/3 c. shortening
6–7 tbsp. cold water

Stir together flour and salt in a mixing bowl. Using a knife or pastry blender, cut in shortening until mixture forms pieces the size of small peas. Sprinkle 1 tablespoon of cold water over part of the mixture; gently toss with a fork. Push moistened pastry to the side of bowl; repeat until all is moistened. Shape dough into a ball. Divide dough in half.

On a lightly floured surface, flatten half of dough. Roll dough out, from the center to the edges, to form a 12-inch circle. Wrap pastry around a rolling pin and transfer to a 9-inch pie plate, being careful not to stretch the pastry. Trim pastry so that 1/2 inch overlaps the pan. Fill pie shell with filling.

Roll out remaining half of dough. Cut into 1/2-inch wide strips. Weave strips on top of filling to make a crisscross crust. Press ends of pastry strips into the rim of crust. Fold bottom pastry over the strips, seal, and flute. Bake as directed in recipe.

Easy Eggnog Pie

2 small pkgs. vanilla pudding mix
2 c. eggnog
1 1/4 c. milk
1/8 tsp. ground nutmeg
1 tbsp. rum (optional)
1 (9-inch) pie shell, baked
whipped topping

Combine pudding mix, eggnog, milk, and nutmeg in a saucepan. Cook and stir over medium heat until mixture comes to a full boil. Remove from heat. Add rum, if desired, and cool 5 minutes, stirring twice. Pour into pie shell. Cover surface with plastic wrap. Chill at least 3 hours. Garnish with whipped topping and pecans. Store leftover pie in refrigerator.

Old-Fashioned Holiday Eggnog Pie

Crust:
1 (15-oz.) pkg. refrigerated pie crust
1 egg, separated
1/8 tsp. red food coloring
1/8 tsp. green food coloring

Filling:
1 envelope unflavored gelatin
1 1/2 c. eggnog, divided
1 c. confectioners' sugar
1/4 c. butter or margarine, softened
1 lb. cream cheese, softened
1/4 tsp. nutmeg
1/2 tsp. rum extract

Preheat oven to 450°F.

Allow crust to stand at room temperature for 20 minutes. Prepare the pie crust as package directs for a one-crust baked shell using a 9-inch pie pan. Trim dough even with edge of the pan.

Make a decorative edge by using a sharp knife and a leaf pattern to cut 16 leaves from the remaining crust. From dough scraps, shape twenty-four 1/4-inch balls. Beat egg white in a small bowl. Brush the edge of crust with egg white. Brush bottoms of leaves and balls with egg white and arrange them around the crust edge to resemble holly leaves and berries.

Place half of the egg yolk in each of 2 cups. Add red food coloring to one and green food coloring to the other; mix well. With a small brush, paint the leaves and berries. Bake for 9–11 minutes, or until lightly browned. Cool completely.

In a small saucepan, sprinkle gelatin evenly over 1/2 cup of eggnog. Let stand for 1 minute to soften gelatin. Cook over medium heat, stirring constantly, until gelatin is dissolved. Remove from heat; set aside.

In a large mixing bowl, combine confectioners' sugar, butter, and cream cheese. Using an electric mixer, beat at low speed until light and fluffy. Gradually add nutmeg, rum extract, gelatin mixture, and remaining eggnog. Beat on high speed until smooth. Refrigerate 15 minutes, or until mixture mounds slightly when stirred; pour into cooled baked shell. Refrigerate until firm, about 4 hours. Sprinkle with additional nutmeg, if desired. Store in refrigerator.

Makes 10 servings.

Pumpkin Pie

3/4 c. sugar
1/2 tsp. salt
1/4 tsp. ground cloves
1 tsp. cinnamon
1/2 tsp. ginger
2 eggs
1 3/4 c. pumpkin, cooked and mashed
1 can (12 oz.) evaporated milk
1 (9-inch) pie shell, unbaked

Preheat oven to 425°F. Combine sugar, salt, cloves, cinnamon, and ginger. In a large mixing bowl, beat eggs lightly. Stir in pumpkin and spice mixture. Gradually add evaporated milk, stirring well. Pour into pie shell. Bake for 15 minutes. Reduce heat to 350°F and bake an additional 40–50 minutes, or until toothpick inserted in center comes out clean.

Sour Cream Raisin Pie

1 1/2 tbsp. cornstarch
1 c. plus 2 tbsp. sugar
3/4 tsp. ground nutmeg
1/4 tsp. salt
1 1/2 c. sour cream
1 1/2 c. raisins
1 tbsp. lemon juice
3 egg yolks
Brown Sugar Meringue (recipe follows)
Pie Pastry (recipe follows)

In a 2-quart saucepan, combine cornstarch, sugar, nutmeg, and salt. Stir in sour cream. Add raisins, lemon juice, and egg yolks; mix. Cook over medium heat, stirring constantly, until mixture thickens and boils. Continue to boil and stir 1 minute.

Pour into baked pie shell. Prepare meringue, and spread it over filling, sealing meringue to crust edges to prevent shrinkage and weeping.

Bake at 400°F for 10 minutes, or until golden. Serve warm; store leftovers in the refrigerator.

Makes 8 servings.

Brown Sugar Meringue:
3 egg whites
1/4 tsp. cream of tartar, packed
6 tbsp. brown sugar
1/2 tsp. vanilla extract

In a 2 1/2-quart bowl, beat egg whites and cream of tartar until foamy. Gradually beat in brown sugar, 1 tablespoon at a time. Continue beating until stiff and glossy. Do not under beat. Beat in vanilla extract.

Pie Pastry (for a 9-inch pan):
1 1/4 c. all-purpose flour
1/2 tsp. salt
1/3 c. shortening
3–4 tbsp. cold water

Stir together flour and salt in a mixing bowl. Using a knife or pastry blender, cut in shortening until mixture forms pieces the size of small peas. Sprinkle 1 tablespoon of cold water over part of the mixture; gently toss with a fork.

Push moistened pastry to the side of bowl; repeat until all is moistened. Shape dough into a ball.

On a lightly floured surface, flatten dough. Roll dough out, from the center to the edges, to form a 12-inch circle. Wrap pastry around a rolling pin and transfer to a 9-inch pie plate, being careful not to stretch the pastry. Trim and flute edges.

Generously prick the bottom and edges with a fork.

Bake at 450°F for 10–12 minutes, or until golden brown. Cool in the pan on a wire rack.

Sweet Potato Pie

1 pkg. (15 oz.) refrigerated pie crust
2 medium sweet potatoes
1 c. sugar
1 c. brown sugar, firmly packed
1/3 c. butter or margarine
3/4 c. milk
1 tsp. nutmeg
1 tsp. vanilla extract
2 eggs, slightly beaten

Preheat oven to 425°F.

Follow package directions to prepare a pie crust for a one-crust filled pie using a 9-inch pie pan. Flute edges to stand 1/2 inch above the rim.

Boil sweet potatoes in a small amount of water until soft; drain. Peel and mash. Place 1 1/2 cups of mashed sweet potatoes in a large bowl. Using a wire whisk, stir in remaining ingredients until well blended. Pour filling into the prepared pastry-lined pie pan. Bake for 10 minutes. Reduce heat to 350°F and bake for an additional 50–60 minutes, or until filling is set and knife inserted in the center comes out clean. To prevent excessive browning, cover edges of crust with strips of aluminum foil. Allow to cool before serving.

Makes 8 servings.

Shoo-Fly Pie

1 c. flour
2/3 c. dark brown sugar
2 tbsp. butter
1/2 tsp. salt
1 egg
1 c. molasses or dark corn syrup
3/4 c. boiling water
1/2 tsp. baking soda
1 (10-inch) deep-dish pie crust, or 2
  (9-inch) pie crusts, unbaked

Preheat oven to 425°F.

Combine flour, brown sugar, butter, and salt in a small bowl until mixture is crumbly; set aside.

In a medium bowl, beat the egg. Gradually stir in the molasses, blending until well mixed.

In a separate small bowl, combine baking soda and boiling water; stir to dissolve. Add the baking soda mixture to the molasses mixture; stir until well blended. Pour into the pie crust(s). Sprinkle flour mixture crumbs evenly over top of the liquid (some will sink and some will float). Bake at 425°F for 10 minutes. Reduce heat to 375°F and bake an additional 35 minutes. Cool to room temperature and serve.

Cheesecakes & Tortes

Fold:
To gently combine two mixtures using a spatula in a light, circular motion.

Glaze:
To give food a shiny coating by applying a thin layer of syrup, beaten egg, or milk.

Chocolate Heaven Cheesecake

1 1/2 c. graham cracker crumbs
1/3 c. sugar
1/3 c. butter or margarine, melted
2 pkgs. (8 oz. each) cream cheese, softened
1/2 c. cocoa
3/4 c. sugar
2 eggs
1 tsp. vanilla extract
1 c. chocolate chips
8 oz. sour cream
2 tbsp. sugar
1 tsp. vanilla extract

Preheat oven to 375°F.

For the crust, combine graham cracker crumbs and sugar. Stir in melted butter. Press along the bottom and halfway up the sides of a 9-inch springform pan.

Blend cream cheese, cocoa, and 3/4 cup of sugar until light and fluffy. Add eggs and 1 teaspoon of vanilla extract, beating until smooth. Stir in chocolate chips. Pour mixture into prepared pan. Bake at 375°F for 20 minutes. Remove from oven and allow to cool in the pan on a wire rack for 15 minutes.

Increase oven temperature to 425°F.

Blend sour cream, 2 tablespoons of sugar, and 1 teaspoon of vanilla extract until smooth. Spread over the cake. Bake for 10 minutes. Remove from the oven and cool in the pan on a wire rack. Loosen sides of pan with a blunt knife or spatula. When cake is completely cool, remove sides of pan. Chill before serving. Refrigerate leftovers.

Plum Torte

1 c. sugar
1/2 c. butter
1 c. flour, sifted
1 tsp. baking powder
2 eggs
12 plums, halved
1 tsp. sugar
1 tsp. lemon juice
1 tsp. cinnamon

Preheat oven to 350° F. Cream sugar and butter. Add flour, baking powder, and eggs. Beat well. Spoon batter into 9-inch springform pan. Arrange plum halves face down in batter. Sprinkle lightly with sugar and lemon juice, depending on the sweetness of the fruit. Sprinkle on cinnamon. Bake 1 hour. Batter will rise and cover plums. Remove and cool to lukewarm before serving with vanilla ice cream or whipped cream.

German Apple Torte

1 egg
3/4 c. sugar
1/2 c. flour
1 tsp. baking powder
1/2 tsp. salt
1 c. apples, peeled and diced
1/2 c. chopped walnuts
1 tsp. vanilla extract

Beat egg with an electric mixer until light and lemon colored. Gradually beat in sugar until mixture is thick and pale. Mix flour, baking powder, and salt; gently fold into egg mixture. Stir in apples, walnuts, and vanilla. Generously butter an 8-inch square pan; pour in batter. Bake at 350° F for 35–40 minutes, or until top is golden brown and crunchy. Serve warm.

Cheesecake à la Orange

Crust:
3/4 c. finely crushed graham crackers
1/2 c. all-purpose flour
1/2 c. finely chopped pecans
1/2 c. butter, melted
1/4 c. sugar

Filling:
3 pkgs. (8 oz. each) cream cheese, softened
2/3 c. sugar
3 eggs
1 1/2 tsp. grated orange peel
1/3 c. orange juice

Glaze:
1/2 c. orange marmalade
1/4 c. white grape juice or orange juice
3 tbsp. Grand Marnier or other orange liqueur
2 tsp. cornstarch
1 1/4 c. seedless grapes, halved

Prepare crust by stirring together crushed graham crackers, flour, pecans, butter, and 1/4 cup sugar. Press into the bottom of a 9-inch springform pan. Place on a shallow baking pan and bake at 350°F for 8 minutes.

To prepare filling, beat cream cheese and 2/3 cup of sugar in a large mixing bowl with an electric mixer at medium–high speed until fluffy. Add eggs, orange peel, and orange juice all at once. Beat on low speed until just combined. Pour over baked crust.

Bake at 350°F for 35–40 minutes, or until center appears almost set when shaken gently. Allow to cool for 15 minutes. Gently loosen the sides of pan. Cool 30 minutes more, then remove sides of pan. When completely cool, cover and chill for 4–24 hours.

One hour before serving, prepare the glaze by combining the marmalade, juice, orange liqueur, and cornstarch in a saucepan. Cook and stir until bubbly, then cook and stir for 2 minutes more. Remove from heat and chill. Immediately before serving, arrange grape halves on top of the cheesecake. Drizzle with glaze.

Makes 12–14 servings.

Individual Coffee Tortes

1 egg yolk
1 tbsp. sugar
1 tsp. vanilla extract
9 oz. cream cheese, softened
3/4 c. strong black coffee
1 tbsp. coffee liqueur
12 thin trifle sponges
1–2 tbsp. unsweetened cocoa powder

Combine egg, sugar, and vanilla extract in a bowl and mix until it has a creamy consistency. Fold in cheese until creamy.

In a separate bowl, combine the coffee and coffee liqueur. Dip sponges briefly in coffee mixture, so that they absorb some liquid, but remain firm and in one piece.

In 4 individual serving dishes, alternate layers of biscuit and cheese mixture, beginning with biscuit and ending with cheese. Dust each with cocoa. Chill in refrigerator until set, about 1 hour.

Paradise Cheesecake

Coconut Crust (recipe follows)
2 envelopes unflavored gelatin
3/4 c. sugar, divided
1 can (6 oz.) pineapple juice
3 eggs, separated
3 pkgs. (8 oz. each) cream cheese, softened
1/4 c. dark Jamaican rum, or 2 tsp. rum extract
1/4 tsp. coconut extract
1 can (20 oz.) crushed pineapple, undrained
2 tbsp. sugar
1 tbsp. cornstarch

Prepare Coconut Crust; set aside. In a saucepan, mix gelatin and 1/2 cup sugar. Add pineapple juice, and let stand for 1 minute. Heat mixture over low heat until gelatin dissolves (about 5 minutes). Remove from heat. Add egg yolks, one at a time, beat well after each addition. Allow to cool slightly.

Beat cream cheese until fluffy. Add gelatin mixture, along with rum and coconut extract; blend well. Chill quickly by setting mixture over a bowl of ice water. Stir until thickened slightly.

In a separate bowl, beat egg whites until foamy. Gradually add 1/4 cup sugar and beat until stiff peaks form. Fold into gelatin mixture. Turn all into prepared crust. Refrigerate overnight.

Before serving, combine undrained pineapple, 2 tablespoons sugar, and cornstarch. Cook, stirring continuously, until mixture boils and thickens. Cool. Spoon over cheesecake.

Coconut Crust
1 1/2 c. vanilla wafer crumbs
1 c. flaked coconut
1/3 c. butter or margarine, melted

Mix vanilla wafer crumbs and coconut. Stir in butter. Press along the bottom and sides of 8- or 9-inch springform pan. Chill until ready to use.

Pumpkin Torte

Crust
24 graham crackers, crushed
1/4 lb. butter, melted
3 tbsp. sugar

Layer 1
2 eggs
8 oz. cream cheese
1/2 c. sugar

Layer 2
1 lb. canned pumpkin
1/2 c. sugar
1/2 c. milk
3 eggs, separated
1 tsp. pumpkin pie spice
1 pkg. unflavored gelatin
1/4 c. water
1/4 c. confectioners' sugar
whipped cream

Mix graham cracker crumbs, melted butter, and sugar. Pat into 9 x 13-inch pan. For first layer, beat eggs, cream cheese, and sugar. Pour over crumbs and bake 20 minutes at 350º F.

In a saucepan, mix pumpkin, sugar, milk, beaten egg yolks, and pie spice. Cook until mixture bubbles. Mix the gelatin with the water and add to the hot pumpkin mixture. Mix and let cool. Beat egg whites until stiff, add the confectioners' sugar, and fold into the cooked mixture. Pour over baked crust and serve with whipped cream.

Creamy Kahlua Cheesecake

Zwieback Crust (recipe follows)
2 envelopes unflavored gelatin
1/2 c. Kahlua
1/2 c. water
3 eggs, separated
1/4 c. sugar
1/8 tsp. salt
2 pkgs. (8 oz. each) cream cheese
1 c. whipping cream
shaved or curled semi-sweet chocolate

Prepare Zwieback Crust.

Dissolve gelatin in Kahlua and water in the top of a double boiler. Beat in egg yolks, sugar, and salt. Cook over boiling water, stirring constantly, until mixture is slightly thickened.

In a large bowl, cream cheese until it is light and fluffy. Gradually beat in Kahlua mixture; allow to cool.

Beat egg whites until they are stiff but not dry. In a separate bowl, beat whipping cream until it is stiff. Fold egg whites and whipped cream into cheese mixture. Pour into prepared pan. Chill in the refrigerator for 4–5 hours, or overnight. Remove from refrigerator 15 minutes before serving. Decorate with shaved or curled chocolate. Makes 12 servings.

Zwieback Crust:
1 1/2 c. fine Zwieback crumbs
1/3 c. sugar
1/3 c. butter, melted

Blend all ingredients together. Press along bottom and halfway up sides of a 9-inch springform pan. Bake at 350°F for 8–10 minutes. Cool.

Marbled Cheesecake

1/3 c. semi-sweet miniature chocolate chips
1 graham cracker crust
2 pkgs. (8 oz. each) cream cheese, softened
1/2 c. cooked or canned pumpkin
1/2 c. sugar
1/2 tsp. vanilla extract
1/2 tsp. cinnamon
dash cloves
dash nutmeg
2 eggs
whipped cream, chopped pecans, or chocolate
  shavings for garnish (optional)

Sprinkle a few of the chocolate chips on the bottom of the pie crust. Melt the remaining chocolate chips in the microwave.

In a large bowl, beat the cream cheese, pumpkin, sugar, vanilla extract, and spices until well blended. Add eggs and mix well.

Remove 1/3 cup of cream cheese mixture, and stir it into the melted chocolate. Pour the remaining cream cheese mixture into the prepared pie crust. Spoon chocolate mixture on top. Use a knife to swirl the two mixtures, creating a marbled effect. Bake at 350°F for 40 minutes, or until center is almost set. Refrigerate at least 3 hours, or overnight. Garnish with whipped cream, chopped pecans, or chocolate shavings.

Makes 8 servings.

PBJ Cheesecake

1 c. graham cracker crumbs
3 tbsp. sugar
2 tbsp. butter or margarine
2 pkgs. (8 oz. each) cream cheese, softened
1 c. sugar
1/2 c. chunky peanut butter
3 tbsp. flour
4 eggs
1/2 c. milk
1/2 c. grape jelly

To make crust, combine graham cracker crumbs, 3 tablespoons sugar, and butter. Press into the bottom of a 9-inch springform pan. Bake at 325°F for 10 minutes.

For filling, combine cream cheese, 1 cup of sugar, peanut butter, and flour in a large mixing bowl. Beat at medium speed using an electric mixer until well blended. Batter should be stiff. Add eggs, one at a time, blending well after each addition. Blend in milk. Pour batter into prepared crust. Bake at 450°F for 10 minutes. Reduce oven temperature to 250°F and bake for an additional 40 minutes. Use a spatula or blunt knife to loosen cake from sides of pan. Cool completely before removing pan. Heat jelly, stirring until smooth; drizzle over cheesecake. Chill until ready to serve.

Makes 10–12 servings.

Chocolate Raspberry Decadence Torte

Chocolate Mousse Cake (recipe follows)
1–2 tbsp. raspberry jelly or seedless jam, room temperature
Chocolate Bands (recipe follows)
1 c. heavy cream
1 tbsp. confectioners' sugar
1/2 tsp. vanilla extract
Raspberry Sauce (recipe follows)

Prepare the Chocolate Mousse Cake and allow it to cool. Brush raspberry jelly lightly around the sides of the cake.

Wrap the sides of the cake with one of the chocolate bands, wavy side up (the jelly will act as a glue). Peel off the wax paper. Attach the second chocolate band, overlapping if necessary, so that the cake is completely encircled.

Combine the cream, sugar, and vanilla extract; whip just until stiff. Place half of the whipped cream atop the cake. Using the back of a large spoon, form a shallow depression in the whipped cream. Fill depression with 3/4 cup of Raspberry Sauce. Serve with the remaining whipped cream and sauce on the side.

Chocolate Mousse Cake:

1 lb. bittersweet or semi-sweet chocolate, coarsely chopped
2 sticks unsalted butter, cut into tablespoons
6 eggs, lightly beaten

Preheat oven to 425°F. Wrap the outside of an 8-inch springform pan with two layers of foil to prevent seepage. Butter pan and line bottom with parchment or wax paper. Butter the paper.

Combine the chocolate and butter in a large metal bowl over a pan of hot, but not simmering, water. Make sure that the bottom of the bowl does not touch the water. Let stand, stirring occasionally, until the chocolate is smooth and melted.

Place the eggs in a large bowl set over simmering water. Stir constantly until eggs are warm to the touch, about 3 minutes. Remove from heat. Using an electric mixer, beat the eggs until they are tripled in size and soft peaks form when the beater is lifted (about 5–8 minutes).

Fold half of the beaten eggs into the melted chocolate until partially blended. Add the remaining eggs and fold until just blended and no streaks remain. Immediately pour into the prepared pan and smooth the surface with a spatula. Place in a large roasting pan and add enough hot water to reach about two-thirds up the sides of the springform pan.

Bake for 5 minutes. Place a piece of lightly buttered aluminum foil over top of the springform, then bake 10 minutes more. Remove the cake from the oven and cool, in the pan, on a rack for 45 minutes. Cover and refrigerate until chilled and very firm, about 3 hours.

To remove cake from pan, slide a small, blunt knife or spatula around the edge and remove the sides of the springform. Gently invert the cake on to a plate covered with plastic wrap, then remove the bottom of the pan.

Peel off the paper. Re-invert the cake on to a cardboard round or cake plate. Cover and refrigerate for 6 hours, or overnight, until thoroughly chilled.

Chocolate Bands:
3 1/2 oz. bittersweet or semi-sweet chocolate

Cut two 13 x 2-inch strips of wax paper. Melt the chocolate and pour 1/4 of it in a strip down the middle of each piece of wax paper.

Using a spatula, spread the chocolate evenly over the paper strips until they are completely covered. Let set, then repeat with remaining chocolate to make a second layer. Allow to stand until firm but still malleable. Using a small, sharp knife, cut a scalloped ripple along one long side of each chocolate strip. Keep the wax paper in place until after the bands have been wrapped around the cake.

Raspberry Sauce:
2 pkgs. (23 oz. each) individually quick-frozen raspberries, thawed
1/3 to 1/2 c. sugar
2 tsp. fresh lemon juice

Drain the berries, reserving the juice. In a small saucepan, warm the juice over low heat. Add 1/3 cup of sugar and lemon juice; stir until the sugar dissolves, about 2 minutes.

Purée the raspberries in a blender. Press through a sieve to remove the seeds.

Stir the raspberry syrup into the purée. Sweeten with remaining sugar to taste. Refrigerate, covered, for up to 1 week.

Peanut Butter and Chocolate Torte

1 c. graham cracker crumbs
1/4 c. brown sugar, firmly packed
1/4 c. unsalted butter, melted
2 c. creamy peanut butter
2 c. granulated sugar
2 pkgs. (8 oz. each) cream cheese, softened
2 tbsp. butter, melted
1 tsp. vanilla extract
1 1/2 c. heavy cream, whipped
3/4 c. semi-sweet chocolate pieces
3 tbsp. butter
1/4 c. sour cream
1/2 tsp. vanilla extract
1 1/2 c. confectioners' sugar, sifted

For crust, combine graham cracker crumbs, brown sugar, and 1/4 cup butter. Press into a 9-inch springform pan.

For filling, beat peanut butter, granulated sugar, cream cheese, 2 tablespoons melted butter, and 1 teaspoon vanilla extract in a large bowl until smooth and creamy. Fold in whipped cream. Spoon into crust. Refrigerate 6 hours.

For topping, place chocolate and 3 tablespoons butter in the top of a double boiler; melt over low heat. Cool 10 minutes. Mix in sour cream and 1/2 teaspoon vanilla extract. Gradually add confectioners' sugar, beating by hand until mixture is smooth and spreadable. Spread over filling. Chill until firm.

Espresso Cream Torte

Torte:
2 (1/2-inch thick) layers classic génoise, or 9-inch diameter sponge cake
1/2 c. hot strong espresso coffee, divided
dash rum, divided
4 tbsp. sugar, divided
18 egg yolks, divided
2 c. sugar, divided
3 lb. mascarpone cheese (an Italian cream cheese), softened, divided
3 c. whipping cream, chilled, divided
Espresso Sauce (recipe follows)
cocoa

Line bottom of a 9-inch springform pan with a layer of génoise 2 1/2 inches up the sides. In small bowl, combine 1/4 cup espresso, rum, and 2 tablespoons sugar; stir until sugar dissolves. Cool. Brush over génoise. Do not drench the génoise layer. In large metal bowl, combine 9 egg yolks and 1 cup sugar. Set over a pan of simmering water, and whisk until just warm to the touch, about 3 minutes. Remove from heat and, using a mixer, beat until pale yellow and tripled in volume, about 5 minutes. Fold in half of cheese.

In separate bowl, whip 1 1/2 cups cream until stiff peaks form. Gently fold cream into egg yolk mixture. Pour over génoise and smooth top. Cover with plastic wrap and freeze until firm, about 6–8 hours. Repeat steps for preparing cheese mixture. Then repeat layers so that there is a layer of génoise, cheese mixture, génoise, cheese mixture. Refreeze. Soften in refrigerator 30 minutes before serving. Garnish with Espresso Sauce and sifted cocoa on top.

Espresso Sauce:
1/4 c. hot strong espresso coffee
3 tbsp. sugar
1 c. whipping cream, chilled

Combine espresso and sugar. In a separate bowl, beat the whipping cream until stiff peaks form. Gently fold the cream into the espresso mixture. Makes 12 servings.

Double Chocolate Mousse Creation

1/3 c. unsalted butter
2 squares unsweetened chocolate
1 c. sugar
2 eggs, well beaten
2/3 c. unbleached flour
1/2 tsp. baking powder
1/4 tsp. salt
1 tsp. vanilla extract
Chocolate Mousse Filling (recipe follows)
1 c. heavy cream

Preheat oven to 350°F. Grease and flour an 8- or 9-inch square baking pan; set aside.

In the top of a double boiler, melt butter and chocolate over hot water. Remove from heat. Add sugar and eggs, mixing well.

Sift together flour, baking powder, and salt. Add to chocolate mixture, stirring well.

Stir in the vanilla extract. Pour into prepared pan. Bake for 25–30 minutes, or until cake is baked but still very moist. Allow to cool.

Remove cake from pan. Cut cake into strips that are approximately as wide as the height of the sides of a 2-quart soufflé dish.

Cut each strip through the center to separate into two thinner halves. Line the bottom and sides of the soufflé dish with the cake strips. (Don't worry; the gaps won't show.)

Spoon Chocolate Mousse Filling into the cake-lined dish. Wrap the dish well, and chill overnight in the refrigerator.

To serve, remove the cake from the pan by first loosening the sides with a knife. Dip the pan partly in hot water to further loosen the cake. Invert on a serving plate.

Whip the cream until stiff, and spread it over the top and part of the sides of the cake. Cut into small slices and serve.

Chocolate Mousse Filling:
1 1/2 lb. semi-sweet chocolate
1/2 c. strong coffee
3 eggs, separated
1/2 c. coffee liqueur
1/2 c. heavy cream

In the top of a double boiler, melt the chocolate and coffee over hot water. Remove from heat.

In a separate bowl, beat the egg yolks until they are pale in color. Stir the egg yolks into the chocolate mixture. Stir in coffee liqueur. Allow mixture to cool.

Beat the egg whites until they are stiff but not dry. In a separate bowl, whip the cream until it is stiff. Gently fold the egg whites and cream into the chocolate mixture.

Makes 12 servings.

Chocolate Truffles Torte

bread crumbs
13 oz. semi-sweet chocolate, divided
2 oz. unsweetened chocolate
3 tbsp. flour
2 c. pecans, finely ground
2 1/2 sticks butter, softened, divided
3/4 c. sugar
7 egg yolks, divided
5 egg whites
pinch salt
2 tbsp. butter, room temperature
1 tbsp. plus 1 tsp. rum or cognac
cocoa

Preheat oven to 350°F. Butter a 9-inch springform pan. Dust lightly with bread crumbs.

In the top of a double-boiler, melt 4 ounces of the semi-sweet chocolate with all of the unsweetened chocolate. Allow to cool slightly.

Stir together flour and pecans in a small bowl.

In a separate mixing bowl, cream 1 1/2 sticks of butter.

Add sugar gradually, beating with an electric mixer on medium-high speed for 1–2 minutes.

Add 5 egg yolks, one at a time, beating well after each addition.

Add the chocolate mixture using an electric mixer on low speed. Gradually add the pecan mixture.

Beat the egg whites with salt until they are stiff, but not dry. Stir in a small amount of the chocolate mixture, then gradually fold in the remaining chocolate.

Turn into the prepared pan, leveling batter by rotating pan rapidly. Bake for 1 hour.

Allow to cool for 15 minutes, then carefully remove pan and cool completely.

For the truffles, in the top of a double boiler, melt 3 ounces of semi-sweet chocolate.

Briskly whisk in 2 tablespoons of butter, 1 egg yolk, and 1 teaspoon of rum.

Drop mixture in 10 mounds on wax paper. Let stand for 45–60 minutes, or until firm enough to handle.

Coat hands with cocoa, roll each mound into a ball, and roll in cocoa.

For the frosting, in the top of a double boiler, melt 6 ounces of semi-sweet chocolate. In a small bowl, cream 1 stick of butter.

Beat in chocolate, 1 egg yolk, and 1 tablespoon of rum. Beat briefly with an electric mixer on high until color lightens slightly.

Frost cooled cake, arrange chocolate truffles on top.

Pastries & Candies

Grease:
To apply a thin layer of butter, shortening, or oil to a pan or other equipment to prevent foods from sticking.

Knead:
To work dough into a uniform mixture by pressing, folding, stretching, and turning.

California Fig Pastries

Pastry:
3 c. all-purpose flour
1 c. sugar
1/4 c. cornstarch
1 1/2 c. butter, cut into 1-inch pieces

Filling:
2 eggs
1 c. brown sugar, firmly packed
1/2 c. orange juice
3 tbsp. lemon juice
1 tsp. grated lemon peel
1 tsp. vanilla extract
2 c. California dried figs, stems removed
1 c. pitted dates
1 c. walnuts

For pastry, combine flour, sugar, and cornstarch in a food processor. Add butter and process until dough holds together. Divide into thirds. Roll out two-thirds of the dough on a 13 x 17-inch baking sheet to reach all corners evenly. Prick with a fork. Bake at 350°F for 15 minutes.

While dough is baking, roll out remaining dough between two sheets of wax paper to form a rectangle about half the size of the baking sheet. Cut dough into 1/4-inch wide strips; set aside.

For filling, combine eggs, brown sugar, orange juice, lemon juice, lemon peel, and vanilla extract in a large bowl, mixing well. Place figs, dates, and walnuts in a food processor or blender and process until finely minced. Add to filling mixture, blending well. Spread filling over baked pastry. Top with pastry strips, crisscrossing them diagonally. Bake at 350°F for 30 minutes, or until pastry strips are lightly browned. Allow to cool and cut into bars. Makes 6 dozen pastries.

Chocolate Mocha Tart

1 (15-oz.) pkg. refrigerated pie crust

Crumb Layer:
1/2 c. crisp coconut cookie crumbs (3–4 cookies)
2 tbsp. flour
2 tbsp. brown sugar
1 tsp. instant coffee crystals
3 tsp. butter or margarine

Filling:
1 c. confectioners' sugar
3 oz. cream cheese, softened
1 1/2 tsp. vanilla extract
2 oz. unsweetened chocolate, melted
2 c. whipping cream
6–8 chocolate-covered candied coffee beans
 or crushed coconut cookies (optional)

Preheat oven to 450°F. Prepare pie crust as package directs for a one-crust baked shell. Place prepared crust in either a 10-inch tart pan with removable bottom or a 9-inch pie pan. Press crust along bottom and up the sides of pan. If necessary, trim edges. Prick with a fork several times.

Combine 1/2 cup cookie crumbs, flour, brown sugar, and instant coffee in a small bowl. Using fork or pastry blender, cut in butter until mixture is crumbly. Sprinkle over crust. Bake for 12–16 minutes, or until light golden brown. Cool completely.

In a large bowl, beat confectioners' sugar, cream cheese, and vanilla extract until well blended. Add chocolate and beat until smooth. Slowly add whipping cream, beating until stiff peaks form. Spread filling into cooled, baked shell. Refrigerate 2–3 hours. Remove sides of pan, and garnish with coffee beans or crushed coconut cookies. Store in refrigerator. Makes 12 servings.

Peach Cranberry Tart

1 (15-oz.) pkg. refrigerated pie crust

Filling:

1 c. fresh or frozen cranberries, thawed
1 lb. frozen sliced peaches, thawed and drained
1/2 c. sugar
1/2 c. dried currants
2 tbsp. flour
1 tsp. almond extract

Streusel:

1/3 c. flour
3 tbsp. brown sugar
2 tbsp. butter or margarine
3 tbsp. sliced almonds

Place a cookie sheet in the oven, and heat oven to 400°F. Prepare the pie crust as package directs for a one-crust filled pie. Place prepared crust in either a 10-inch tart pan with removable bottom or a 9-inch pie pan. Combine all filling ingredients in a large bowl; mix well. Pour into crust.

For streusel, combine flour and brown sugar; mix well. Using a knife or pastry blender, cut in butter until mixture is crumbly. Stir in almonds. Sprinkle over fruit mixture. Place on preheated cookie sheet. Bake at 400°F for 30–40 minutes, or until hot and bubbly around edges.
Makes 10 servings.

Almond Plum Tart

Pastry:

1 1/4 c. all-purpose flour
2 tsp. sugar
1/2 tsp. salt
1/3 c. shortening
3–4 tbsp. cold water

Filling:

1 c. finely ground almonds
1/3 c. sugar
1 egg
1/2 tsp. finely shredded lemon peel
1/2 tsp. ground cinnamon
1/4 tsp. almond extract
8–10 plums, halved and pitted
2 tbsp. butter
1/3 c. currant jelly, melted

For pastry, combine flour, 2 teaspoons sugar, and salt. Using a knife or pastry blender, cut in shortening until mixture forms pieces the size of small peas. Sprinkle 1 tablespoon of cold water over part of the mixture; gently toss with a fork. Push moistened pastry to the side of bowl; repeat until all is moistened. Shape dough into a ball.

Roll dough out on a lightly floured surface to form a 12-inch circle. Place in a 9–inch quiche dish. Trim edges of dough even with the rim of the pan.

Combine almonds, 1/3 cup sugar, egg, lemon peel, cinnamon, and almond extract in a large mixing bowl. Beat with an electric mixer on low speed until combined. Spread almond mixture evenly in pastry shell. Place plums, cut side down, on top of almond mixture. Dot with butter.

Bake at 375°F for 50 minutes, or until crust is brown and juice from plums is nearly evaporated. Cool on wire rack. Brush top with melted jelly.

Makes 6–8 servings.

Gingerbread Pear Cake

3/4 c. butter, softened, divided
1 c. brown sugar, divided
3 ripe pears, peeled, cored, and thinly sliced
1 egg
1/4 c. dark molasses
1 1/2 c. all-purpose flour
2 tsp. ground ginger
1 tsp. cinnamon
1/4 tsp. nutmeg
1/4 tsp. cloves
3/4 tsp. baking soda
1/4 tsp. salt
1/3 c. boiling water, mixed with 1 tsp. vanilla extract
1/2 c. heavy whipping cream
1/4 c. confectioners' sugar
1 tsp. vanilla extract

Preheat oven to 350°F. Lightly grease a 9-inch round or square baking pan.

Heat 1/4 cup butter and 1/2 cup brown sugar in a large skillet, stirring often until sugar melts. Add pear slices and continue to cook, stirring often, until pears begin to soften. Pour into prepared baking pan and set aside.

In a large bowl, cream the remaining butter and brown sugar until light and fluffy, about 1 minute. Add egg and molasses, beating until well blended.

Sift the flour, ginger, cinnamon, nutmeg, cloves, baking soda, and salt together. Fold into the creamed butter mixture, alternating with boiling water, being careful not to over mix.

Spoon batter over the pears in the baking pan. Bake for 35–40 minutes, or until cake springs back when lightly touched. Cool, in the pan, on a wire rack for 5 minutes. Invert on a serving platter. Slice and serve with whipped cream.

For whipped cream, beat the heavy cream, confectioners' sugar, and vanilla extract until soft peaks form.

Perfect Pralines

1 1/2 c. dark brown sugar
1 1/2 c. granulated sugar
2 tbsp. margarine
1/8 tsp. salt
1 1/2 c. evaporated milk
2 c. whole pecans
1 tsp. vanilla extract

In a large saucepan, combine all ingredients. Bring to a slow boil over medium-low heat, stirring continuously with a wooden spoon. Boil for 4 minutes, or until mixture reaches 260°F. Remove from heat and stir briskly for 2 minutes, or until mixture cools, thickens, and becomes creamy.

On large pieces of wax paper, aluminum foil, or oiled cookie sheets, drop 2 or 3 pecans with about 1 tablespoon of mixture for each praline. Cool thoroughly. Store in an airtight container.

Makes 40 two-inch pralines.

Divinity

2 1/2 c. sugar
1/2 c. light corn syrup
1/2 c. water
1/4 tsp. salt
2 egg whites
1 tsp. vanilla extract
1 c. chopped nuts

Combine sugar, syrup, water, and salt in a 2-quart saucepan. Cook over medium heat until boiling. Reduce heat and boil until temperature reaches 248°F.

In a separate bowl, beat egg whites until stiff. Beating constantly, slowly pour half of the hot syrup over the egg whites.

Cook remaining syrup until it reaches a temperature of 272°F. Pour into the egg white mixture. Beat until mixture begins to lose its gloss. Stir in vanilla extract and nuts. Drop by teaspoonfuls on wax paper.

Makes 1 1/2 pounds.

Peanut Butter and Chocolate Drops

1 c. butter or margarine
1/2 c. creamy peanut butter
2 1/3 c. graham cracker crumbs
2 c. confectioners' sugar, sifted
2 c. flaked coconut
1 c. chopped walnuts
6 oz. semi-sweet chocolate chips
1 (2 1/2-inch) piece paraffin, chopped

Combine butter and peanut butter in a 2-quart saucepan. Cook over medium heat, stirring constantly, until melted. Remove from heat and set aside.

Combine graham cracker crumbs, confectioners' sugar, coconut, and walnuts in a bowl. Add peanut butter mixture and toss until well blended.

Line a cookie sheet with wax paper. Shape mixture into 1/2-inch balls and place on cookie sheet. Cover with aluminum foil and chill in the refrigerator.

Combine chocolate chips and paraffin in the top of a double boiler. Place over hot water, stirring until melted. Dip each of the peanut butter balls, one at a time, into the chocolate.

Line cookie sheets with fresh wax paper. Place balls on cookie sheets and let stand until the chocolate is set. Cover with aluminum foil and store in the refrigerator.

Makes 2 pounds of drops.

Royal Rum Balls

2 tbsp. cocoa
2 c. confectioners' sugar, divided
2 1/2 c. finely crushed vanilla wafers
1 c. finely chopped pecans
3 tbsp. light corn syrup
1/4 c. rum

Sift cocoa and 1 cup confectioners' sugar together in a large bowl. Mix in all remaining ingredients, except 1 cup of confectioners' sugar. Shape into 1-inch balls. Sprinkle remaining confectioners' sugar on a plate and roll the balls in it to coat. For best flavor, store in a tin for at least 1 week before eating. These candies will keep up to 1 month.

Makes 36 rum balls.

Chocolate Truffles

3 pkgs. (6 oz. each) semi-sweet chocolate chips
1 can sweetened condensed milk
1 tbsp. vanilla extract
finely chopped nuts, flaked coconut, sprinkles, cocoa, or confectioners' sugar for coating

Heat the chocolate chips along with the condensed milk in a heavy saucepan, over low heat. When chocolate is melted, remove from heat and stir in vanilla extract. Chill 2 hours, or until firm. Shape into 1-inch balls and roll in desired coating. Chill 1 hour, or until firm. Store covered at room temperature.

Makes about 6 dozen truffles.

Apricot Truffles

1 1/4 c. hazelnuts
1/4 c. finely chopped dried apricots
24 oz. white chocolate chips, divided
6 tbsp. heavy cream

Spread hazelnuts in a thin layer on a baking sheet. Bake at 350°F for 8–10 minutes, or until nuts are light brown and the dark skins are cracked. Rub nuts with a cloth to remove as much of the skins as possible. Place nuts in a food processor and process until finely chopped.

In a 1-quart glass container, combine cream and half the chocolate chips. Microwave on medium for 3–4 minutes, stirring twice, until chocolate is melted and smooth. Stir in apricots and 3/4 cup chopped hazelnuts. Cover and refrigerate for 1–2 hours, or until mixture is firm enough to hold its shape.

Remove mixture from refrigerator and shape into 1 1/4-inch balls. Place balls on a cookie sheet lined with wax paper. Refrigerate for 1 hour, or until firm.

Place remaining white chocolate in a small dish and microwave on medium for 3–4 minutes, stirring often, until chocolate is melted and smooth. Using tongs, dip each truffle, one at a time, into the melted chocolate. Tap on edge of the dish to remove excess chocolate. (If chocolate begins to harden, microwave a few seconds to re-melt it.) Place on a cookie sheet lined with wax paper. Before chocolate hardens, sprinkle with some of the remaining chopped hazelnuts. Serve in paper candy cups. Truffles can be stored in an airtight container up to 2 weeks in the refrigerator or 1 month in freezer. Makes 28 truffles.

Ice Cream Creations

Sift:
To put dry ingredients, such as flour, through a sifter or sieve.

Stir:
To mix ingredients with a spoon using a circular motion.

Chocolate Mint Baked Alaska

Crust:
1/2 c. chocolate mint chips
3 tsp. butter
1 1/2 c. chocolate wafer crumbs

Filling:
1 c. chocolate mint chips
2 tbsp. corn syrup
2 tbsp. heavy cream
3 pt. vanilla ice cream, softened

Meringue:
4 large egg whites
1/2 tsp. cream of tartar
3/4 c. sugar

For crust, combine 1/2 cup chocolate mint chips and butter in a double boiler over hot, but not boiling, water. Stir until chips are melted and smooth. Add chocolate wafer crumbs; stir until well blended. Press into the bottom of a 9-inch springform pan; freeze until firm.

For filling, combine 1 cup chocolate mint chips, syrup, and heavy cream over hot, but not boiling, water. Stir until chips are melted and smooth. Remove from heat and cool to room temperature.

In a large bowl, whip the ice cream until it is smooth but not melted. Gradually stir in chocolate mixture (flecks will appear in ice cream). Spoon into the center of the crust, mounding high in the center and leaving a 3/4-inch edge. Using a spatula, smooth ice cream over to form a dome. Freeze until firm. Remove sides of pan.

Preheat oven to 450°F.

For meringue, combine egg whites and cream of tartar in a large bowl. Beat until soft peaks form. Gradually add sugar and continue to beat until stiff peaks form. Spread meringue over ice cream and crust to cover completely; swirl to decorate. Bake at 450°F for 4–6 minutes, or until lightly browned. Serve immediately.

Makes 12 servings.

Fruity Ice Cream Cake

1 (10-in.) angel food cake
1 pkg. lime-flavored gelatin
1 pkg. strawberry-flavored gelatin
1 pkg. orange-pineapple-flavored gelatin
1 pkg. frozen strawberries, partially thawed
1/2 gal. vanilla ice cream, softened
1 can crushed pineapple, drained
1 can mandarin oranges

Cut cake into thirds. Tear each third into bite-size pieces, placing each third in a separate bowl. Sprinkle one bowl with dry lime-flavored gelatin mix, one with strawberry, and one with orange-pineapple. Toss until cake pieces are evenly coated.

Place strawberry cake pieces in a 10-inch tube pan. Spoon strawberries over top. Spread evenly with 2 2/3 cups of ice cream. Next, layer the lime cake pieces of top. Spoon pineapple over these. Spread with another 2 2/3 cups of ice cream. Layer on orange cake pieces. Spoon on mandarin oranges. Top with a final layer of 2 2/3 cups of ice cream.

Cover all tightly with aluminum foil. Freeze at least 2 days. Unmold on a chilled plate. Let stand at room temperature for 10–15 minutes. Slice and serve. Makes 15 servings.

Frozen Gingerbread Roll

1/2 c. hazelnuts
6 large eggs, separated
2 tbsp. butter or margarine, softened
3/4 c. dark brown sugar, packed
1 1/2 tsp. ground cinnamon
1 tsp. ground ginger
pinch of ground cloves
2 tbsp. dark molasses
1/4 c. brewed coffee, room temperature
3/4 c. all-purpose flour
1/2 tsp. baking powder
confectioners' sugar
2 pt. rum raisin ice cream, slightly softened
caramel topping, warmed (optional)

Preheat oven to 350°F. Line a 15 1/2 x 10 1/2-inch jelly roll pan with wax paper. Butter and lightly flour the paper.

Spread hazelnuts in a baking pan. Bake for 8–12 minutes, stirring occasionally, until fragrant and lightly browned. While hazelnuts are still hot, turn them out on a towel. Fold towel over nuts and rub off as much of the papery brown skins as possible. Allow to cool completely; then process in a food processor until finely ground.

Place the egg yolks in a large bowl. Add butter, brown sugar, cinnamon, ginger, and cloves. Beat with an electric mixer on medium speed for 1 minute until smooth. Add molasses and coffee; beat 1 minute more until well blended.

In a small bowl, combine flour, baking powder, and 1/4 cup ground hazelnuts until blended. Stir into yolk mixture.

With clean, dry beaters, beat the egg whites until stiff, but not dry, peaks form when beaters are lifted. Do not over beat. Spoon 1/4 of the whites on to the yolk mixture and gently stir until blended. Fold in half of remaining whites, and then all of the remaining whites. Pour batter into the prepared pan. Spread gently and evenly. Sprinkle with remaining ground hazelnuts. Bake 12–15 minutes, or until a toothpick inserted in the center comes out clean.

While cake is baking, generously sprinkle a clean kitchen towel with confectioners' sugar. When the cake is done, invert the hot cake on the towel. Remove the pan and carefully peel off the paper. Using the towel, roll up the cake from the long side, jelly roll style. Let cool completely.

Carefully unroll the cake. Working quickly, spoon softened ice cream to within 1 inch of one long edge. Roll up cake, starting from covered edge. Place on a cookie sheet. Cover tightly with plastic wrap and freeze until firm, at least 8 hours and up to 1 week.

When ready to serve, pour a small amount of caramel topping on individual cake plates. Cut gingerbread log into 1-inch thick slices; place on sauce and serve.

Fried Mexican Ice Cream

1 pt. vanilla ice cream, or other favorite flavor
1/2 c. crushed corn flakes or cookie crumbs
1 tsp. ground cinnamon
2 tsp. sugar
1 egg
oil for deep frying
honey
whipped cream

Scoop out 4 balls of ice cream and place them in the freezer.

In a bowl, combine corn flake crumbs, cinnamon, and sugar. Roll frozen ice cream balls in crumb mixture and freeze again.

Beat the egg. Dip ice cream balls in the egg and then in remaining crumb mixture. Refreeze until ready to use. (If a thicker coating is preferred, dip once more in egg and then in crumb mixture.)

When ready to serve, heat oil to 350°F. Place 1 frozen ice cream ball in fryer basket and lower into hot oil for 1 minute. Immediately remove and place on an individual serving dish. Drizzle with honey and top with whipped cream. Fry ice cream balls one at a time. Dessert should be crunchy on the outside and just beginning to melt on the inside.

Makes 4 servings.

Peach Ice Cream

1 c. peaches
1 1/4 c. sugar, divided
2 tbsp. cornstarch
1/4 tsp. salt
2 c. milk
2 large eggs
1 tbsp. vanilla extract
2 c. light cream

In a food processor or blender, coarsely chop the peaches. Combine peaches and 1/4 cup sugar; chill.

In a separate bowl, combine cornstarch, salt, and 1 cup sugar. Gradually blend in milk. Microwave on high for 8 minutes, or until thick, stirring 2–3 times during cooking. Beat the eggs and slowly add them to the cornstarch mixture, stirring constantly. Microwave on high for 2 minutes, or until thick and creamy. Chill.

Add vanilla extract and cream to the mixture. Stir in peaches. Place in an ice cream freezer and freeze according to the manufacturer's directions.

Makes 10 servings.

Chocolate Mint Ice Cream Pie

1 qt. vanilla ice cream
2 tbsp. creme de menthe
1 square (1 oz.) semi-sweet baking
  chocolate, grated
1/2 c. crushed peppermint candy
1 (9-inch) graham cracker crust

Place ice cream in a large mixing bowl. Cut into squares. Microwave on low 3–4 minutes, or until softened. Add creme de menthe, chocolate, and half of peppermint candy. Beat at medium speed until smooth. Spoon into crust. Sprinkle with remaining candy. Freeze for 5 hours, or until firm.

Makes 8 servings.

Cookies & Snack Cakes

Whip:
To beat rapidly to increase the volume of an ingredient such as cream or egg whites.

Zest:
To remove the outmost skin of citrus fruit with a knife, peeler, or zester. Be careful not to remove the pith (the white layer between the zest and the flesh), which is very bitter.

Simply Sugar Cookies

3 c. all-purpose flour
1 tsp. baking soda
1 c. unsalted butter, softened
1 c. sugar
1 tsp. vanilla extract
1 egg

Preheat oven to 375° F. Sift flour and baking soda together; set aside.

Cream together butter, sugar, and vanilla extract in a large bowl. Add the egg; beat until mixture is light and fluffy. Gradually stir in the flour mixture. Divide dough in half. Wrap both halves in plastic wrap and refrigerate for 1 hour.

Roll out half of dough on a lightly floured surface until it is 1/4 inch thick. Cut out cookies using a floured cookie cutter. Repeat with remaining dough. Place cookies on an ungreased cookie sheet. Bake for 8–10 minutes, or until golden. Remove from cookie sheet and place on a wire rack to cool. Decorate with icing, sprinkles, or colored sugar, if desired. Makes 3 dozen cookies.

Double Chocolate Nut Cookies

1 c. butter or margarine, softened
1 1/3 c. granulated sugar
2/3 c. brown sugar, packed
2 large eggs
2 tsp. vanilla extract
3 1/2 c. all-purpose flour
1 tsp. baking powder
1 tsp. baking soda
pinch salt (optional)
1 c. semi-sweet chocolate, chopped
1 c. white chocolate, chopped
1 c. macadamia nuts, chopped

Preheat oven to 375°F. In a large bowl, cream together butter, granulated sugar, and brown sugar until light and fluffy. Add eggs and vanilla extract; mix for 2 minutes more. Blend in flour, baking powder, soda, and salt.

Stir in the chocolates and macadamia nuts. Shape into 1-inch balls. Place 2 inches apart on ungreased cookie sheets. Bake for 10–12 minutes. Allow to cool on wire racks. Makes 3 dozen cookies.

Chewy Oatmeal Cookies

3/4 c. butter flavored solid shortening
1 1/4 c. light brown sugar, firmly packed
1 egg
1/3 c. milk
1 1/2 tsp. vanilla extract
3 c. quick cooking oats
1 c. all-purpose flour
1/2 tsp. baking soda
1/2 tsp. salt
1/4 tsp. cinnamon
1 c. raisins
1 c. chopped walnuts

Heat oven to 375° F. Grease baking sheet. Combine shortening, light brown sugar, egg, milk, and vanilla in large bowl. Beat at medium speed with electric mixer until well blended. Combine oats, flour, baking soda, salt, and cinnamon. Mix into creamed mixture at low speed just until blended. Stir in raisins and nuts. Drop by rounded tablespoonfuls 2 inches apart on a baking sheet. Bake for 10–12 minutes, or until lightly browned. Cool 2 minutes on baking sheet.

Chocolate Raisin Cookies

1/2 c. butter or margarine, softened
1 c. sugar
1 egg
1 c. applesauce
2 1/2 c. flour
2 tbsp. cocoa
1 tsp. baking powder
1/2 tsp. baking soda
1/2 tsp. salt
1 tsp. cinnamon
1 c. raisins
1 c. nuts (optional)

Cream together butter and sugar. Stir in egg and applesauce. Sift together flour, cocoa, baking powder, soda, salt, and cinnamon. Add to butter mixture. Stir in raisins and nuts, if desired. Drop by teaspoonfuls on a lightly greased cookie sheet. Bake at 350°F until done.

Fruits and Nuts Cookies

1 lb. butter or margarine, softened
1 c. granulated sugar
1 c. brown sugar
1 tsp. vanilla extract
3 eggs
5 c. flour
1 tsp. baking soda
pinch salt
2 c. whole pitted dates
2 c. whole candied cherries, red and green
2 c. whole pieces candied pineapple
2 c. whole pecans
2 c. whole walnuts
2 c. whole Brazil nuts

Cream together the butter, sugar, and vanilla extract. Add the eggs, one at a time, beating well after each addition. Stir in flour, baking soda, and salt. Stir in fruits and nuts. Divide dough into 4 equal parts and shape into rolls of the desired size. Wrap in aluminum foil and chill for several hours. Dough will keep in the refrigerator for several weeks. Slice and place on a cookie sheet. Bake at 350°F for 10–12 minutes.

Almond Fruit Cookies

2 1/2 c. flour
3/4 c. brown sugar, firmly packed
1/2 c. sugar
2 tsp. cinnamon
1/2 tsp. soda
1/2 tsp. cream of tartar
1 c. butter or margarine, softened
1 tbsp. grated orange peel
1 tsp. vanilla extract
1 egg
1 c. chopped almonds
1 c. chopped, pitted dates or prunes

Preheat oven to 350°F.

In a large bowl, combine all ingredients except almonds and dates. Using an electric mixer, blend on low speed until well mixed and a dough forms. Stir in almonds and dates. Shape dough into 1-inch balls. Place 2 inches apart on ungreased cookie sheets. Bake for 12–15 minutes, or until edges are a light golden brown. Allow to cool 1 minute before removing from cookie sheet.

Fruit Jewels

1 c. all-purpose flour, sifted
1 tsp. baking powder
1/2 tsp. salt
2 tsp. ground cinnamon
1/2 tsp. ground nutmeg
1/4 tsp. ground cloves
1/4 c. butter or margarine, softened
1/2 c. brown sugar, packed
1 tbsp. orange peel, grated
1/2 c. evaporated milk, undiluted
2 c. mixed candied fruit, chopped
1 c. walnuts, coarsely chopped
1 c. (6 oz.) semi-sweet chocolate pieces
1 c. seedless raisins

Preheat oven to 375°F.

Sift together flour, baking powder, salt, cinnamon, nutmeg, and cloves; set aside.

Cream butter. Slowly add brown sugar, creaming well. Stir in orange peel. Add one-third of flour mixture and half of evaporated milk, mixing well. Add half of remaining flour mixture and all of remaining evaporated milk; mixing well. Add remaining flour mixture; mixing well. Stir in all remaining ingredients. Drop by heaping teaspoonfuls on to lightly greased cookie sheets. Bake for 12 minutes. Allow to cool in a wire rack.

Banana Cookies

3 medium-size, ripe bananas
1/3 c. peanut or safflower oil
1 tsp. vanilla extract
1/8 tsp. salt
1 1/2 c. rolled oats
1/2 c. uncooked oat bran
1 1/2 c. dried fruits (dates, apricots, raisins), coarsely chopped
1/2 c. walnuts or almonds, chopped

Preheat oven to 350°F. Grease 2 cookie sheets.

Mash bananas in a large bowl until smooth (should yield about 1 1/2 cups). Stir in oil, vanilla extract, and salt. Add oats, oat bran, fruits, and nuts; mix well.

Drop by rounded teaspoonfuls about 1 inch apart on cookie sheets. Using the back of a spoon, flatten each cookie slightly.

Bake for 20–25 minutes, or until bottom and edges are golden. Cool completely; store in the refrigerator. Makes 2 dozen cookies.

White Drop Cookies

1 c. shortening
3 c. sugar
1 tsp. baking soda, dissolved in 1/4 c. sour milk
4 eggs
4 tsp. baking powder
1 c. milk
1 tsp. vanilla
5 1/4 c. flour
1/4 tsp. nutmeg

Cream sugar and shortening. Combine remaining ingredients in order listed, stirring well after each addition. Drop by teaspoonfuls on cookie sheets, and bake 350º F for 10–12 minutes. Cool on cookie sheet for 10 minutes before removing to serving plate.

Fruit-Filled Cookies

3 c. brown sugar
1 1/2 c. butter or margarine
3 eggs
1 tbsp. vanilla extract
4 c. flour
1 tsp. soda, dissolved in 1 tbsp. warm water

Filling:
1/2 c. raisins
1/4 lb. dates, chopped
1/2 c. crushed pineapple with juice
sugar
cornstarch

Combine brown sugar, butter, eggs, vanilla extract, flour, and soda dissolved in water; mix well.

Shape dough into rolls. Wrap in wax paper and refrigerate for 24 hours.

About 2 hours before ready to bake, prepare filling. Cook raisins in water for 10 minutes. Add dates and pineapple with juice. Add sugar to taste. Thicken filling with cornstarch as needed. Chill before using.

Cut cookie dough rolls into slices about 1/8 inch thick. Spoon filling on half of the slices. Top with the remaining slices. Bake at 350°F for 10–12 minutes, or until golden.

Tropical Fruit Bars

3 c. rolled or quick oats
1 c. unsweetened flaked coconut (optional)
1 c. oat flour
1/2 c. chopped nuts
1 c. orange juice
1 banana, mashed
1 tsp. salt
1 can (20 oz.) unsweetened, crushed pineapple
2 c. chopped dates

Preheat oven to 350°F.

Mix all ingredients together, except pineapple and dates.

Add more orange juice if needed to hold mixture together. Firmly press half of mixture into the bottom of 9 x 12-inch glass baking dish.

Stir together pineapple and dates.

Cook until thickened. Spread over oat mixture in dish. Top with remaining oat mixture.

Bake for 30 minutes.

TIP: To make oat flour, blend regular rolled oats at high speed in a blender.

Cherry Bars

4 c. vanilla wafers, crushed
1/2 c. butter, melted
1 c. chopped pecans
1/2 c. red candied cherries
1 can sweetened condensed milk

Preheat oven to 350°F. Stir together wafer crumbs and butter. Press into the bottom of a 9 x 11-inch baking dish.

Mix cherries and pecans, then spread over crumb base. Pour condensed milk over top of all. Let stand for 10 minutes. Bake for 25 minutes. When cool, cut into bars.

Makes 2 dozen bars.

Fruit Cocktail Snack Bars

2 eggs
1 1/2 c. sugar
1 can (1 lb. 1 oz.) fruit cocktail, undrained
2 1/4 c. flour
1 1/2 tsp. soda
1/2 tsp. salt
1 tsp. vanilla extract
1 1/3 c. flaked coconut
1/2 c. chopped nuts

Glaze:
3/4 c. sugar
1/2 c. butter
1/4 c. evaporated milk
1/2 tsp. vanilla extract

Preheat oven to 350°F.

In a large mixing bowl, beat eggs and sugar at high speed until light and fluffy. Add fruit cocktail, flour, soda, salt, and vanilla extract. Beat at medium speed until well blended. Pour into a 15 x 10-inch greased baking dish. Sprinkle with coconut and nuts. Bake for 20–25 minutes, or until golden brown.

While bars are baking, combine ingredients for glaze in a saucepan. Bring to a boil and boil for 1 minute. Drizzle over bars as soon as they are removed from the oven.

Black-Bottom Cherry Bars

1 pkg. (6 oz.) chocolate chips
1/4 c. butter or margarine
4 c. slightly crushed corn flakes
1 c. golden or dark raisins
1 c. chopped red candied cherries
3/4 c. peanuts
1 can (14 oz.) sweetened condensed milk

Preheat oven to 350°F. Grease a 9 x 13-inch pan.

Melt chocolate chips and butter in a small saucepan over low heat, stirring occasionally. Spread evenly in the bottom of the greased pan. Refrigerate until set.

In large bowl, combine the corn flakes, raisins, cherries, peanuts, and condensed milk until well coated. Press firmly in the pan over the chocolate layer. Bake at 350°F for 17–20 minutes, or until edges begin to bubble and top is golden. Allow to cool, then refrigerate until set. Cut into bars. Store in the refrigerator.

Chocolate Banana Brownies

1 c. all-purpose flour
1/3 c. unsweetened cocoa
1/4 c. nonfat dry milk powder
1/4 tsp. baking soda
1/4 tsp. salt
1 large, very ripe banana
1 c. sugar
2 large egg whites
1/4 c. buttermilk
1 tsp. vanilla extract

Preheat oven to 350°F. Coat a 9-inch square baking pan with nonstick cooking spray.

In a large mixing bowl, combine flour, cocoa, milk powder, soda, and salt in a bowl; set aside.

In a food processor or blender, purée banana, sugar, egg whites, buttermilk, and vanilla extract until smooth. Add dry ingredients and pulse until just blended. Pour into prepared pan. Bake for 25 minutes, or until toothpick inserted in center comes out just clean. Cool on a wire rack. When completely cool, cut into 2-inch squares.

Makes 16 servings.

Chocolate Chip Brownies

2 1/4 c. flour, unsifted
2 1/2 tsp. baking powder
1/2 tsp. salt
3/4 c. butter or margarine, softened
1 1/4 c. granulated sugar
1 1/4 c. brown sugar, packed
1 tsp. vanilla extract
3 eggs
12 oz. chocolate chips

Preheat oven to 350°F. Grease a 15 x 10 x 1-inch baking pan.

Combine flour, baking powder, and salt in a bowl; set aside.

In a large bowl, cream butter, sugars, and vanilla extract. Add eggs, one at a time, creaming after each addition. Gradually beat in flour mixture. Add chocolate chips. Spread evenly into prepared pan. Bake for 35–40 minutes. Cool in pan. When completely cool, cut into pieces.

Makes 6 servings.

Candied Popcorn Snack Cake

1/4 c. butter
1/4 c. oil
2 1/2 c. marshmallows
20 caramels
10 c. popcorn
1 c. peanut M&Ms
1 c. peanuts

In a double boiler, melt butter, oil, marshmallows, and caramels. In a large pan, mix popcorn, M&Ms, and peanuts. Pour caramel mixture over this and mix to coat well. Pour into a greased Bundt pan, and let stand until set.

Index

Cakes 5
Apricot Almond Cream Cake 14
Blueberries and Cream Cake 11
Bourbon Cake 13
Chocolate Marshmallow Cake 6
Classic Chocolate Pound Cake 9
Cream Cheese Carrot Cake 10
German Chocolate Cake 8
Gumdrop Cake 12
Lemon Poppy Cake 10
Mississippi Mud Cake 6
Moist Blueberry Cake 14
Peanut Butter and Chocolate Cake 7
Peanut Butter Spice Cake 8
Pineapple Upside-Down Cake 11
Pound Cake 9
Quick and Easy Chocolate Cake 6
Royal Cake 12
Rum Cake 13

Strawberries 15
Berry Bliss 16
Strawberries and Cream Celebration 17
Strawberries with Yogurt Sauce 16
Strawberry Buttercream Cake 18
Strawberry Dessert Topping 18
Strawberry Candy 17
Strawberry Pie 16

Apples 19
Apple Brown Betty 22
Apple Cranberry Pie 22
Apple Crumbles 20
Apple Pie 20
Apple Raisin Squares 21
Apple Roll 20
Baked Apples 22
Old World Apple Tart 21

Cobblers & Fruits 23
Apples and Prunes Cobbler 25
Bananas Foster 26

Basic Fruit Cobbler 24
Cherry Surprise 24
Creamy Orange Fruit Dip 24
Fried Bananas 26
Nutty Bananas 25
Peach Cobbler 24
Pineapple Bake 26
Pineapple Banana Treat 26

Pies 27
Banana Cream Pie 31
Boston Cream Pie 29
Easy Eggnog Pie 33
Fudge Pie 28
German Chocolate Pie 32
Lemon Chess Pie 30
Lemon Meringue Pie 30
Lime Pie 31
Old-Fashioned Holiday Eggnog Pie 34
Pecan Pie 28
Pumpkin Pie 34
Raisin Crisscross Pie 33
Raspberry Peach Melba Pie 32
Rocky Road Pie 31
Shoo-Fly Pie 36
Sour Cream Raisin Pie 35
Sweet Potato Pie 36
Turtle Pie 28

Cheesecakes & Tortes 37
Cheesecake à la Orange 39
Chocolate Heaven Cheesecake 38
Chocolate Raspberry Decadence Torte 42
Chocolate Truffles Torte 46
Creamy Kahlua Cheesecake 41
Double Chocolate Mousse Creation 45
Espresso Cream Torte 44
German Apple Torte 38
Individual Coffee Tortes 39
Marbled Cheesecake 41
Paradise Cheesecake 40
PBJ Cheesecake 42

Peanut Butter and Chocolate Torte 44
Plum Torte 38
Pumpkin Torte 40

Pastries & Candies 47
Almond Plum Tart 49
Apricot Truffles 52
California Fig Pastries 48
Chocolate Mocha Tart 48
Chocolate Truffles 52
Divinity 51
Gingerbread Pear Cake 50
Peach Cranberry Tart 49
Peanut Butter and Chocolate Drops 51
Perfect Pralines 50
Royal Rum Balls 52

Ice Cream Creations 53
Chocolate Mint Baked Alaska 54
Chocolate Mint Ice Cream Pie 56
Fried Mexican Ice Cream 56
Frozen Gingerbread Roll 55
Fruity Ice Cream Cake 54
Peach Ice Cream 56

Cookies & Snack Cakes 57
Almond Fruit Cookies 59
Banana Cookies 60
Black-Bottom Cherry Bars 62
Candied Popcorn Snack Cake 63
Cherry Bars 62
Chewy Oatmeal Cookies 58
Chocolate Banana Brownies 63
Chocolate Chip Brownies 63
Chocolate Raisin Cookies 59
Double Chocolate Nut Cookies 58
Fruit Cocktail Snack Bars 62
Fruit-Filled Cookies 61
Fruit Jewels 60
Fruits and Nuts Cookies 59
Simply Sugar Cookies 58
Tropical Fruit Bars 61
White Drop Cookies 60